GOSPEL
G L I T T E R

LEARNING TO SHINE
IN THE DARKNESS

LINDSAY STONE CORBETT

Gospel Glitter

Trilogy Christian Publishers
A Wholly Owned Subsidiary of Trinity Broadcasting Network
2442 Michelle Drive Tustin, CA 92780

Trilogy Christian Publishing/TBN and colophon are trademarks of Trinity Broadcasting Network. For information about special discounts for bulk purchases, please contact Trilogy Christian Publishing.

Trilogy Disclaimer: The views and content expressed in this book are those of the author and may not necessarily reflect the views and doctrine of Trilogy Christian Publishing or the Trinity Broadcasting Network.

Manufactured in the United States of America
10 9 8 7 6 5 4 3 2 1
Library of Congress Cataloging-in-Publication Data is available.

ISBN: 978-1-64773-823-5
E-ISBN: 978-1-64773-824-2

DEDICATION

to Sandy Finch Stone

Gospel Glitter is dedicated to my late mother, who forever inspired me to sparkle, shine, and stand out. Her extravagance was not only externally evident in her beauty, but also the radiance of God beamed from her spirit.

Mother, you were not perfect (as none of us are) but you knew the Perfector, Author, and Finisher of our faith. You modeled vulnerability to the Word of God through your own redemption story. Although heartache leaves me feeling a vast variety of emotions today, I will choose to renew my mind in the Word of God for the hope of tomorrow.

> Oh death, where is thy sting? Oh grave, where is thy victory?
>
> —1 Corinthians 15:55 (KJV)

What greater way is there to honor your legacy than by shining the light of the Gospel of Jesus Christ for all the world to see? As you rest on heaven's eternal shore, I pray you can see the light of the truth spreading across the darkness of this earth.

Until we unite again in glory,
Your firstborn

TABLE OF CONTENTS

FOREWORD

'You are the light of the world. A town built on a hill cannot be hidden. Neither do people light a lamp and put it under a bowl. Instead they put it on its stand, and it gives light to everyone in the house. In the same way, let your light shine before others, that they may see your good deeds and glorify your Father in heaven.'

—Matthew 5:14-16

Gospel Glitter is a personal testimony in an effort to overcome the carnal nature of mankind. While enduring struggles and sufferings, I am continually learning to shine brighter so that the darkness of this world can see the source of my strength and hope, the Gospel of Jesus Christ. The goal and purpose of this testament is to create a glitter movement that illuminates the one true path to eternal life with Christ. I pray you find encouragement and inspiration to aid your own personal walk of life.

INTRODUCTION

Have you ever felt sad, heartbroken, lonely, depressed, angry, bitter, and felt guilty about it because you are a Christian? I know I have, and I know that God's Word is the only anchor during fluctuating emotional circumstances. Do you feel like there have been times that you have felt that you were in "survival mode"? Meaning, that all you know how to do is survive where you are at physically, mentally, or even spiritually. It has been during these times in my own life that I found myself questioning my faith, my mental health, and my heart.

I realized, through my own suffering and loss, that God's Word is not only the way to survive these dark times in our lives, but also the only way to thrive in such a dark world. The world we live in seems to be getting darker by the minute. Many people, including myself, believed the new decade 2020 would be a fresh start. The new year quickly began to spiral into one of the most challenging times in history.

Early in 2020, though, God spoke the word "glitter" into my spirit.

I thought to myself, *God am I really losing my mind or did I just hear the word "glitter"?*

I then felt God say to me, "Be the glitter."

Merriam-Webster says that glitter is "to shine by reflection with many small flashes of brilliant light, to shine with strong emotion, to be brilliantly attractive, lavish, or spectacular."[1]

God asked me to be the glitter; in other words, shine His light by highlighting His Word to the world. The darkness of 2020 cannot outweigh the light from God's Word. His Word says,

> if my people will humble themselves and pray and turn from their wicked ways, I will heal their land.
>
> —2 Chronicles 7:14 (NIV)

We can all agree that when a container of glitter spills on the floor, that it scatters and shines brighter together and is almost impossible to wipe up. Let's be the glitter together and let His Word be what shines through us!

Let me begin by sharing a little bit about myself and my background. I am from a rural town in eastern North Carolina. I am a daughter of God. God redeemed me and saved me at the early age of seven years old. I had the honor and privilege of growing up in a Christian home with a foundation of deep Christian heritage. I was blessed to come to know the Lord at a young age. I have seen the power of God manifested in generations before me and in my own life. I know God has called me to share the good news of His Gospel so that you too may experience His unconditional love for you.

Women from all walks of life, I cannot wait to share my story with you and how I am learning to combat all my emotions with God's Word. I pray that we can grow together in our spiritual maturity because Jesus has given us the choice to know Him intimately.

SURPRISE

If you read the introduction to this book, you probably did not expect to see "surprise" as the title of this chapter, but it is an emotion that we all have experienced and plays an important part in my story. Merriam Webster dictionary defines surprise as "the feeling caused by something unexpected or unusual."[2] While it is important for us to know the definition of our emotions, it is more important that we do not allow our emotions to define us. Knowing your identity in Christ and the power that resides in God's Word is life-changing. So today if we can start with that foundation of understanding, then we can be open to trusting our heavenly father with our destiny.

Surprise is an emotion that I felt on Christmas Eve of 2011. My husband and I got married in September of 2009, and in 2011 we decided to begin the journey of starting a family. Little did I know the journey that we were about to embark upon. Christmas Eve 2011, I took a home pregnancy test, and to my surprise it was positive. I was overjoyed at the thought of becoming a mother. What better timing—what a great Christmas gift to share the news with close family and friends! We shared the news with a few family members but waited to be safe since I had not been to the doctor to confirm.

On New Year's Eve, my husband Allen and I went out to eat at our favorite Japanese restaurant to celebrate the upcoming New Year. How extremely blessed we felt that God had gifted us a pregnancy and how thankful we were to be able to become parents so quickly. While we were still in the restaurant, I noticed that I felt some pain in my lower abdomen. The pain worsened, so I felt like it would be best to head home; maybe I just needed to rest. We got home, the pain became severe, and I quickly realized I was miscarrying.

My surprise quickly became a heartache. I kept thinking; *I do not understand, why is this happening?* The scripture, "And we know that all things work together for good to those who love God, to those who are the called according to His purpose" came to my remembrance (Romans 8:28, KJV). Honestly, I thought, *how can miscarriage be good? What good could come from this?*

That same night, once I finally dozed off to sleep, I got the call from my best friend's husband stating that they were on the way to the hospital because she was in labor. My best friend was nine months pregnant and excited about their next chapter as a family. I wanted to be there with her, so I got dressed and headed to the hospital. Soon later, my best friend had a beautiful healthy baby girl. I was so happy for her, but inside there was this immense sadness that I could not explain. I did not share my sadness at the time because who would want to ruin such a joyful moment for this blessed family?

I called my doctor, and I can remember them saying to me that this was very common in first time pregnancies and not to be discouraged, that I was young and healthy and I shouldn't have any further difficulties. Wisdom says, "A man's heart plans his way, but the Lord directs his steps" (Proverbs 16:9, NJKV). Little did I know that my emotional rollercoaster was just getting started.

> Dear friends, do not be surprised at the fiery ordeal that has come on you to test you, as though something strange was happening to you. But rejoice inasmuch as you participate in the sufferings of Christ, so that you may be overjoyed when his glory is revealed.
>
> —1 Peter 4:12-13 (NIV)

Jesus never promised that the road to a victorious life would be easy, but He does promise that He will be with us. We must remember to never let distractions or bumps along the way become distance between us and Him. It is critical, in whatever journey you are on while you are reading this, to get as close to Jesus as possible. Find a Bible that you love and get a highlighter ready because He will illuminate your path through His Word so that you can be victorious in Him!

> Your word is a lamp to my feet and a light for my path.
>
> —Psalm 119:105 (ESV)

HEARTACHE

Heartache has been defined as the anguish of mind or sorrow. To me, heartache felt as though my soul hurt. I could not understand how I was mourning a child that I never saw or held in my arms. Looking back, I can say that my interpretation, at the time of my last conversation with my doctor's office, left me feeling like my sadness was blown off. As if maybe I should not mourn the loss of this pregnancy because, in the world's eyes, pregnancy and fetal life has been taken for granted. Pregnancy and the life of a child have somehow been warped into a "choice" of whether or not the parent is ready to be a mother. I knew what God's Word said,

> Before I formed you in the womb I knew you; before you were born I sanctified you; I ordained you a prophet to the nations.
>
> —Jeremiah 1:5 (NKJV)

It seems as if our culture has taken advantage of the miracle of childbirth. Once you are impregnated, God has already gifted that soul into your hands to nurture and care for. If you do not feel capable of doing so, please reach out for help and allow a family to adopt that precious soul as their own.

> But when God, who set me apart from my mother's womb and called me by His grace, was pleased.
>
> —Galatians 1:15 (BSB)

> My frame was not hidden from You when I was made in secret, when I was woven together in the depths of the earth. Your eyes saw my unformed body; all my days were

written in Your book and ordained for me before one of them came to be.

—Psalm 139:15-16 (BSB)

Children are a gift and a heritage, and abortion has never been and will never be God's idea. Even though now the world has hardened their hearts to this practice of pro-choice, God's heart breaks every time someone chooses to kill that miracle. I pray that God will have mercy on us as a nation for the apathetic nature that we have had regarding abortion.

Maybe you are reading this, and you have already had an abortion. Even still, God still loves you, and He is willing to forgive you. It is easy to be misinformed in our world today with the constant blasts of headlines that confuse right with wrong.

Woe to those who call evil good and good evil, who put darkness for light and light for darkness, who put bitter for sweet and sweet for bitter."

—Isaiah 5:20 (NIV)

I have no desire to judge or condemn anyone who has had an abortion. In God's eyes, all sin is equal. I am not perfect, nor do I profess to be. We have all fallen short of the glory of God but praise God for His abundance of mercy and grace.

My little children, I am writing these things to you so that you may not sin. But if anyone does sin, we have an advocate with the Father, Jesus Christ the righteous.

—1 John 2:1 (ESV)

As a nation, it is imperative that we stand against laws and regulations that contradict God's Word. Proverbs 17:15 (NLT) states, "Acquitting the guilty and condemning the righteous—both are detestable to the LORD."

I believe we are living in the last days and that God has called each of us for such a time as this, to be a light in the darkness. If you look in Revelation 2:5 (ESV) it says, "Remember therefore from where you have fallen; repent, and do the works you did at first. If not, I will come to you and remove your lampstand from its place, unless you repent."

If you have suffered a miscarriage, it is okay to feel the emotion of grief, and everyone processes pain or grief differently. At the time, no one around me felt my pain in the same way. The only person I could go to was God.

> "Come to Me all who are weary and heavy laden and I will give you rest for My yoke is easy and My burden is light."
>
> —Matthew 11:28–30 (NIV)

God was all I knew, and at the time I was even a little angry with Him. The passionate belief that abortion is contradictory to God's will fueled my lack of understanding and trusting God through this miscarriage. Like I said before, I could not understand, and likely never will, why God allowed me to miscarry when there are so many babies being killed every day by abortion. God's Word says that He already knows how we feel, and He knows the desires of our hearts. I decided I would just let Him know verbally how I felt in a casual conversation through prayer with Him.

If you have a need today or your heartache feels that it hurts to the core of your being, trust me, sound it out and tell God out loud. I cried out to Him and realized that I would have to stay in constant communion with Him to move forward. There is something freeing about talking to God out loud. His Holy Spirit comes in as promised as a comforter. He makes intercession for us, and our prayers become declarations over our lives and our future. Not only did I start praying openly, but I also went to church frequently, asked for prayer often, and just knew that God would allow me to have children someday.

A few months passed by, and thankfully we saw another

positive pregnancy test. *Wow*, I thought to myself, *our prayers have been answered. This is the moment that we will become parents.* I scheduled an appointment with my doctor, and because of our previous miscarriage they brought us in earlier than normal just to keep a closer eye on me. I remember being so anxious about the appointment. The future can be scary at times because we cannot control our circumstances. I would soon learn that even though I could not control my circumstances, I could control my response to them.

If you are at a crossroads in your life and fearful of taking the next step, I encourage you to stick with God's Word and prayer, but to also have peace because He has good plans for you and He loves you. You are the love of our Lord Jesus' life. He gave His life for you so that He could spend eternity with you. You cannot clean your act up enough to be worthy; He does not require that. Jesus just wants you to rely on His strength right now and breathe, take the step of faith He is calling you to. God's plans are always better than we can think or imagine.

> The Lord is not slow in keeping his promise, as some understand slowness. Instead he is patient with you, not wanting anyone to perish, but everyone to come to repentance.
>
> —2 Peter 3:9 (NIV)

ANXIOUS

Anxiety was an unfamiliar emotion that began creeping into my mind's emotional core and thoughts after my second positive pregnancy test. In the process, I never realized the slow fade that fear was rooting in my mind. Historically, my personality had always been confident of good news, a free spirit, and overall joyful. In fact, when I was in nursing school, my roommates can attest that most of the time I would forget about assignments until the night before and have to study in cram session style, yet I still was not anxious.

Early that morning, my husband and I walked in together to my doctor's office, and of course, we prayed that all would be well with this pregnancy. Even as I recall this moment, I can still feel that heart-pacing sensation in my chest. The medical staff were all very positive at that appointment and felt sure that I would be okay this time. I had a urine pregnancy test that confirmed the pregnancy in their office. Then, they drew labs and gave us the full first-time parent treatment. I got gift bags of pamphlets and the whole "what to expect when you're expecting" experience. The staff was all smiling, yet I was still so fearful that I could not even enjoy the moment.

The next day the office called me and said that my lab work was positive for pregnancy, but according to my timeline of conception, they did not think the levels were rising fast enough. They wanted me to come back the next day to confirm that the levels were increasing. Of course, after that call the anxiety increased within me. My husband and I prayed and begged God to have mercy on us. We read and recited scriptures like,

> 'For I know the plans I have for you,' declares the LORD, 'plans to prosper you and not to harm you, plans to give you hope and a future.'
>
> —Jeremiah 29:11 (NIV)

I can do all things through Christ who strengthens me.

—Philippians 4:13 (BSB)

Looking back, I did not address my anxiety with the scriptures in God's Word about fear. I chose to focus my meditation on scriptures that we felt would protect the baby. I wanted to prove the doctors wrong and experience a miracle.

As I reflect back on this experience, I believe God was wanting me to dig deeper into His Gospel. I think He was desiring for me to become aware and reliant on Him with all of my emotions, not just in my response to bad news.

I went to my appointment the next morning for my lab work. I got a call that afternoon, and the doctor said, "Your labs are not increasing as they should. We believe you may be miscarrying again."

I could not believe it. I was so angry now. I demanded that they check with an ultrasound, and they obliged my request. My husband and my mom came with me, we were believing that they would see a baby when they looked, and that the baby would be there healthy and safe just as we desired.

The medical staff performed the ultrasound, and there was no heartbeat. There was no healthy fetus detected, and it appeared that as the fetus was trying to develop it could not survive. They told me I would probably start bleeding soon and that I was, in fact, miscarrying again.

My choice of an anxious emotional response did nothing to protect my heart from breaking once more. Why is it so easy to choose fear? As humans, especially as adults, we think if we go ahead and imagine the worst-case scenario, we will not be as hurt when our plans do not work out. So maybe anxiety is really just rooted in a lack of control.

Are you fearful right now? Do not make the same mistake I did by ignoring the fear. Deal with the fear head-on. This is definitely not the last time I would experience anxiety. Fear is a liar. Fear cripples you where you are. Fear is not from God.

> The LORD himself goes before you and will be with you; he will never leave you nor forsake you. Do not be afraid; do not be discouraged.
>
> —Deuteronomy 31:8 (NIV)

Believe me, I did not have it all figured out at the moment for sure, but at least I realized fear was my enemy. As I was learning to move on, another emotion called anger quickly began to rear its ugly head in my thought life.

ANGER

What kind of God would allow miscarriage to happen not just once but twice? This question caused anger to bubble up to the surface of my soul. Most people, including myself, have experienced temporary feelings of anger with people, friends, and family. This anger is usually rooted in some form of disappointment or hurt. We can all agree humans are not perfect; therefore, it is no surprise when people make you feel angry. What came as a surprise to me was my response of anger towards a God who *is* perfect. What I could not grasp at the time was the bigger picture that God's will is actually perfect. God's Word says,

> For it is better to suffer for doing good, if that should be God's will, than for doing evil.
>
> —1 Peter 3:17 (ESV)

The phrase, "if that should be God's will" speaks volumes. I cannot always understand God's will for my life, but I must trust that every verse from God's Word is truth. Anger in our flesh may always be difficult to overcome, but when that feeling causes us to commit an immoral act that contradicts the divine law that we confess to believe in, then we are committing a sin. I believe we have to make a choice to renew our minds daily by reading the Gospel.

> Do not be conformed to this world, but be transformed by the renewal of your mind, that by testing you may discern what is the will of God, what is good and acceptable and perfect.
>
> —Romans 12:2 (ESV)

Some critics, scholars, and even some Christians do not believe that God can speak to us individually anymore. Personally, I have felt God speak to me. Scripture affirms in Malachi 3:6 (NKJV) by stating, "For I am the Lord, I do not change." I interpret that to mean if God spoke, saved, or healed in Bible times, then surely He will still do it for His children today.

> Jesus Christ is the same yesterday, today, and forever.
>
> —Hebrews 13:8 (NIV)

Over time, He has taught me to be reliant on Him through my suffering in ways that I will respond by reading His living word and as the Holy Spirit draws me closer. Even still, in this particular moment of my life, I was angry with God. I remember saying to Him, "I have served you with all my heart since my childhood! I followed most of the rules and tried my best to live a perfect life! Why are you doing this to me?" I felt as though God grew silent. I was so desperate to hear His voice again, but I could not stop venting and ranting to Him long enough to hear Him.

> "My sheep know my voice, and I know them. They follow me."
>
> —John 10:27 (CEV)

In His sovereignty, God was not asking for me to be perfect; He just wanted me to be close to Him.

> "If you do this, you will be children who are truly like your Father in heaven. He lets the sun rise for all people, whether they are good or bad. He sends rain to those who do right and to those who do wrong."
>
> —Matthew 5:45 (ERV)

Anger in my soul did not last too long because I loved God too much. I knew that even though this mountain of defeat was before me

God was still good to me. God still loved me. God still had a plan for me. I only knew those things because even when my flesh was weak, I just kept digging for encouragement and seeking divine encounters from Him. I remember through this process several moments of prophetic words being spoken over my husband and I, stating that we would be parents and that God did have a plan and He would carry us through this. I had to cling to these words.

People tried to comfort us but they would fail us repeatedly because people are human and not God. One lady in my home church wrote me a letter and it started out so kind and thoughtful, however in the letter she stated, "Have you ever just thought maybe it is not God's will for you to have a child?"

Seriously? Who is she to think and have the audacity to say this to me? Constantly I had to speak to myself, *people are human, they are not God.* I knew that God birthed my desire to become a mother and conceive a child so I would have to continue to encourage myself with that.

> For to set the mind on the flesh is death, but to set the mind on the Spirit is life and peace.
>
> —Romans 8:6 (ESV)

I remember specifically going to God's Word and finding the stories of the miraculous conceptions of Sarah and Hannah. They defied the odds and God was faithful.

> Delight yourself in the Lord, and he will give you the desires of your heart.
>
> —Psalm 37:4 (ESV)

> For the LORD God is a sun and shield; the LORD bestows favor and honor. No good thing does he withhold from those who walk uprightly.
>
> —Psalm 84:11 (ESV)

The key to this chapter is simply that, no matter what emotion you are feeling or what the world says about you or your future, only rely on the truth of God's Word.

> Make them holy by your truth; teach them your word, which is truth.
>
> —John 17:17 (NLT)

Anger is an emotion that you cannot get stuck in because anger is dangerous. I had to make a choice to forgive without even being asked for forgiveness. The Bible tells us that Jesus has forgiven us, so who am I to hang on to hurts and let that grow a bitter root?

It became critical to the protection of my mental health and soul to make a choice to channel my pain into determination and not give up. I told our doctor that I felt it was time for me to see a specialist.

You will soon discover that when I thought God was the quietest, He was actually working. I would experience and see this as a demonstration of His sovereignty.

> For the LORD will not forsake his people for his great name's sake: because it hath pleased the LORD to make you his people.
>
> —1 Samuel 12:22 (KJV)

HOPEFUL

A month or two after our second miscarriage, I went to my first appointment with a fertility specialist. This doctor ran lots of lab work, and then proceeded to tell us that I would be his easiest patient because my blood work revealed I was already pregnant and that I would just need to take some medication to help sustain this pregnancy. He was positive in his prediction because he could not find any real abnormalities in my lab work. The doctor requested that I come in every forty-eight hours over the next couple weeks.

At that time, I was working as a nurse in a doctor's office. By then, my work family knew all that I was going through and were always cheering me on. My support team was slowly growing all around. I would soon realize how important having a support system would be. Not only would it help me stay encouraged, it would give God a bigger platform to demonstrate His goodness in my life.

I got a call with lab results, my labs seemed to be heading in the right direction, but they still wanted to keep a close eye on me. I went back to the office numerous times, and a few days later I got another call. "Mrs. Corbett, we believe you are miscarrying again."

I could not believe what they were saying. I remember questioning them repeatedly, "Are you sure?"

"Yes," they stated, "but we still think we can help you."

At this point my soul is aching at a much deeper level. I have now experienced a miscarriage for the third time. How can I remain hopeful now?

The mental anguish that I experienced had the potential to become destructive. I can recall, there was a Sunday morning that I told my husband I felt like a clay pot that had been thrown on the ground and broken into a million pieces. I told him that begrudgingly, because he woke up on that Sunday morning—right after the third miscarriage—

and told me we needed to go to church. He asked me and encouraged me to go ahead and get up and get ready.

Listen up men, it is your role to be the spiritual head of the family. Rise up, men of God, and commit your ways to the Lord so you can urge your household to worship God in Spirit and in truth. Ephesians 5:23 (ESV) says,

> for the husband is the head of the wife even as Christ is the head of the church, his body, and is himself its Savior.

Additionally wives, God's Word states,

> In the same way, you wives must accept the authority of your husbands. Then, even if some refuse to obey the Good News, your godly lives will speak to them without any words.
>
> —1 Peter 3:1 (NLT)

In the heat of this moment, I can confess that my thought process started more like; *Seriously,* (emphasizing with a dramatic eye roll and huff of frustration) *I do not want to be around any happy people right now, especially not at church.* I felt like people may have opinions about me like our faith was not strong enough, there must be some hidden sin in our lives, or just maybe they would be discouraged and question their own faith. All of these are entirely human thoughts, but I was going to have a moment and sulk in my own self pity. I rolled my eyes at his encouragement and thought, *well I guess I will just read a devotional since it is Sunday and after all that is what we Christians are supposed to do, at least have some kind of "church" even if it is at home.* I read the online devotional, and I remember just weeping continuously. This was one of those defining moments in my Christian walk. The devotional was so amazingly designed for me in that moment and is too good not to reference.

LINDSAY STONE CORBETT

And I am convinced and sure of this very thing, that He who began a good work in you will continue until the day of Jesus Christ [right up to the time of His return], developing [that good work] and perfecting and bringing it to full completion in you.

—Philippians 1:6 (AMP)

"According to the Bible, God is the Potter, and we are the clay (see Romans 9:20-21). When we first come to the Lord, we are like a hard lump of clay that is not very pliable or easy to work with. But God puts us on His potter's wheel and begins to refashion and remake us so that we can discover the wonderful plan He has for our lives. Sometimes that process of molding is uncomfortable at first. The reason it hurts is because God has to peel away the things in our lives that would keep us distant from Him. So out of His love for us, He keeps working and working on us, trimming away this bad attitude and that wrong mind-set, carefully reshaping us until gradually we are changed into the likeness of His Son Jesus. Don't be discouraged with yourself because you have not yet arrived. The more God works in your life, the closer you are growing in relationship to Him. Enjoy your life each day, even as God is shaping you. Let the Potter do His work, and trust that He has your best interest at heart. You can always trust God that He has your best interest at heart, and all that He does in your life is for your benefit."[3]

I did not go looking for this devotional; it was loaded on my phone, and it was just the one for that day. Wow! I felt God speaking to me directly in that moment. I knew I would have to keep pressing on and holding on to Him in a way like no other. I also believed that I would have to get radical in my faith, yet in my flesh this would be most difficult. We occasionally had what we referred to as "come to Jesus meetings" in our home where we prayed, and physically marched around our home. The biblical story of Joshua's battle at Jericho would resonate as I could imagine the Israelites marching around the wall surrounding the city until it came crashing down, just as God promised.

> When the trumpets sounded, the army shouted, and at the sound of the trumpet, when the men gave a loud shout, the wall collapsed; so everyone charged straight in, and they took the city.
>
> —Joshua 6:20 (NIV)

We had a specific room in our home that we designated and prepared as a nursery for our miracle baby. We were trying to take action with our faith and prepare or envision the promise of God. First Peter 1:13 (NASB) reads,

> Therefore, prepare your minds for action, keep sober in spirit, fix your hope completely on the grace to be brought to you at the revelation of Jesus Christ.

God calls us as His children to prepare and expect miracles. After all, His Word states He is preparing a place for us as well.

> If I go and prepare a place for you, I will come again and receive you to Myself, that where I am, there you may be also.
>
> —John 14:3 (HCSB)

God also emphasizes the importance of the armor of God and refers specifically to this verse,

> ...and having shod your feet with the preparation of the gospel of peace.
>
> —Ephesians 6:15 (NKJV)

One evening amid one of our home prayer meetings, we walked in the nursery and anointed the room with anointing oil, pleading the blood of Jesus over our future child. As we prayed, I can remember physically smelling the scent of baby powder in that empty room. I believed this aroma to be a physical manifestation of the Holy Spirit as a comfort and reassurance that someday a baby would be in that nursery.

We invited close friends that were equally yoked and desired to see the miraculous as we did.

> Do not be unequally yoked together with unbelievers. For what fellowship has righteousness with lawlessness? And what communion has light with darkness?
>
> —2 Corinthians 6:14 (NKJV)

In moments where you are desiring "enter the throne room," so to speak, and receive insight or understanding from God, it is important to gather or partner with believers that are equally assured in the miraculous. I wrote scriptures, many of which I have shared throughout this text, all over the walls and over the doorways of our home on posted sticky notes. I had to stay focused on God's Word and what He had to say in order to survive this emotional turmoil. At some point in your own walk with Christ you too may sense the urgency to "get extreme" with your faith.

I went back to the doctor's office for my follow up appointment following the third miscarriage. The doctor told me that there was a procedure that he could do for me and in addition he would give me injectable hormones to possibly prevent any further miscarriage. I was okay with all of the doctor's recommendations, and we proceeded with their plans. I had the procedure which was a minor surgery and used many different hormonal medications as prescribed and followed up repeatedly; I even had therapeutic acupuncture.

I made a conscious choice to stay hopeful because the God of the universe loved me enough to send His only son to die on the cross for my sins. And as you recall, spoke to me through a devotional in a moment of emotional self-pity. I am so thankful for a God who does not give up on us even when we have already given up on ourselves.

GUARDED

Have you ever been too afraid to be happy because you have witnessed or suffered traumas in your own life? I have learned that the root of being what I would describe as guarded is unbelief. Unbelief is the same as doubt. So many times, I have questioned situations and circumstances because God's Word describes so many promises and miracles. Still, I cannot always see them happening in my own life. To really believe is to believe that God's will in your life is better than your plans.

> "For my thoughts are not your thoughts, neither are your ways my ways," declares the Lord. "As the heavens are higher than the earth, so are my ways higher than your ways and my thoughts than your thoughts."
>
> —Isaiah 55:8-9 (NIV)

I will not pretend that I have it all figured out because, at times, I have still struggled with doubt. Not necessarily doubtful of God's Word, but doubting that those promises and miracles will happen for *me*. So instead of being victorious in my daily walk during this trial, I would just feel as though I was numb—walking through my situation and circumstances just waiting for the ball to drop. I was no longer feeling hopeful and I was so afraid to fully buy into the scripture that states,

> For the LORD God is a sun and a shield; the LORD gives grace and glory; He withholds no good thing from those who walk with integrity.
>
> —Psalm 84:11 (BSB)

Do you ever struggle and think that maybe, if I reserve my excitement and anticipation and my plans fall through, then it will not be as painful? I had already experienced such heartache that I started guarding myself as a protective mechanism. After all, there is a scripture in Proverbs 4:23 (NIV) that says, "above all else, guard your heart, for everything you do flows from it."

Let us look at that scripture again. Guard your heart? I thought I said that the root of guarding was unbelief, but the Bible clearly states to guard your heart? Yes, you are right to guard your heart.

As I reflect on the condition of my heart I realized that I not only guarded my heart but I also guarded my spirit as well. The Bible describes the heart as the wellspring of life. My heart was guarded because I was afraid of the pain, but I was also guarding my spirit, which was rooted in unbelief. I needed to dig further in God's Word to understand that God does not want me walking around in defeat, fearing the future, or walking on eggshells in an effort to guard my heart. Psalm 112:7 (ISB) encourages us by stating, "He need not fear a bad report, for his heart is unshaken, since he trusts in the LORD." God wanted me to pray until my heart would align with His spirit and His will for my life, not my own. The scripture, "create in me a clean heart, O God, and renew a right spirit within me," could not be more applicable to me (Psalm 51:10, KJV). The heart in a human can be deceptive; it can allow you to be held captive by your emotions or circumstances.

I can remember going to the doctor's office and just going through the motions of the checkboxes of things they wanted us to do. I successfully completed all the medical team's recommendations including surgery, hormones, and conception.

Yes, with no trouble after the procedures and medications, we were pregnant yet again. My flesh, by this point, was confused. This was my fourth pregnancy, and I could not relax. We were still praying, still trying so hard to overcome the fear of miscarriage, and still leaning on family members and friends' support. I knew I needed to get past my guarded heart and spirit, but I was bound up in chains of fear.

There is a story in the Bible in the book of Mark 9:20-29 (NIV) that I found when searching God's Word to help me with my guarding and unbelief. The story is about a boy that was captive to an evil spirit.

> Jesus asked the boy's father, "How long has he been like this?"
>
> "From childhood," he answered. "It has often thrown him into fire or water to kill him. But if you can do anything, take pity on us and help us."
>
> "If you can?" said Jesus. "Everything is possible for one who believes."
>
> Immediately the boy's father exclaimed, "I do believe; help me overcome my unbelief!"
>
> Jesus did cast out the spirit, and the boy was healed. Jesus honored the father because he prayed, "help me overcome my unbelief."
>
> —Mark 9:21-25 (NIV)

I began reciting that in my head over and over while I went to my follow up appointments.

HAPPY

Happiness is defined as an emotion when we experience feelings of satisfaction based on our current circumstances. For example, when your team wins the game, you may feel happy.

"Lord, let this pregnancy be the one to make it, let this baby live and not die," I prayed. Lab work results were in, and they confirmed that the pregnancy seemed to be heading in the right direction. The doctors, of course, had me on a tight leash, requiring that I come in every forty-eight hours for lab work. We were so thankful for every good report that we received. My numb composure started to get some feeling back. I started feeling *happy* this time. At eight weeks into this pregnancy, everything seemed to be on track.

I will never forget this moment: I was working, and had my cell phone in my pocket. My phone rang and it was my doctor. They proceeded to say, "The lab work levels are no longer increasing at the appropriate rate, and there is a chance you may be miscarrying again."

This cannot be true. I went into an empty room and shut the door at work and began to weep—not just cry, but weep. One of the doctors that I worked with, who had been watching my emotional rollercoaster of a journey to motherhood, knocked on the door and just walked in. I was broken, and by this time I had slid down on the floor in a puddle of despair. This doctor was not religious and did not confess to be a Christian, and I was afraid that this would just be another way that someone could say, "how can you worship a God who would allow such chaos?"

To my surprise, though, this doctor just picked me up, hugged me, and said, "you will become a mother, you have faith, and it will happen."

I was devastated in that instance, but I was also blown away that those words came from his mouth. Maybe this whole experience was not all for nothing. He and others that I worked with had been watching me, listening to me, and seeing my faith being stretched so thin. Sometimes what we are facing is not about us but about what faith others can see in us. This may be the only way they ever see Jesus in us. After all, His Word says that we are to be the salt and light in the earth (see Matthew 5:13-16, NLT).

The doctors' office scheduled me for an ultrasound because I insisted on knowing if they were right or if they made a false assumption. My husband and my mom were in the room with me praying. The screen came up, and sure enough we saw this beautiful little heartbeat. I can remember lying on my back in a most awkward and vulnerable position in front of my doctor raising my hands and rejoicing for this heartbeat. This is the furthest we had ever gotten, and surely this was the one that would make it.

The doctor never acknowledged my personal praise break. He had this blank look on his face as he kept taking pictures and moving the ultrasound probe around.

I was confused. My heart of momentary happiness started sinking. "What is wrong?" I asked.

The doctor proceeded to say, "I was right, you are still going to miscarry."

I asked, "How can you say that? There is a heartbeat?"

The doctor explained that the sac looked unstable and did not look like it would be a viable pregnancy. He recommended that I take a medication that would go ahead and eliminate the pregnancy because the fetus would not survive on its own.

I remember telling the doctor that I would not take the medication. I could not allow the miracle that God gave me to be aborted based on an opinion. I immediately started looking for a new doctor. I thought, *the nerve of this doctor to minimize my faith and fetal heartbeat miracle.* I could not believe after all the money that we spent and all the ups and downs that this doctor still thought we would miscarry. I refused to accept this death sentence.

We prayed, we begged God, cried, got angry, prayed more, and the cycle went on and on. I soon found a new fertility specialist to take me on as a new patient. I filled her in with my whole story.

She said, "Well, let's have a look by ultrasound today and see what is going on."

This was roughly a week after my last ultrasound. The screen pulled up, and there was still a heartbeat. *See, I knew it!* I was still pregnant, and this baby was still alive.

I am still holding my breath a little because her expression was blank and emotionless just like the other doctor. She told me that she did not believe this pregnancy would survive, and she had little confidence in the development of this baby. She also encouraged me to take the medication that would eliminate the pregnancy.

I still refused. I told her that I would let the miscarriage happen on its own because I believed God would heal it. She likely thought I was crazy, but at this point, I did not even care. I went in week after week for ultrasounds. Still the little fetus, having a heartbeat, but no good reports from my doctor. Finally, we went in for another ultrasound at twelve weeks, and there was no longer a heartbeat.

How could this be, God? This time I was happy. I was hopeful. I believed that You were going to do it.

DEFEATED

Is this the end, God? Will I ever get to be a mother? These are questions that flooded my mind. I felt defeated, and that felt like an understatement. *How could I walk around and tell people that I was miscarrying for the fourth time?* I thought this defeat would destroy my witness to others. I worried that no one would ever think that the God I served was real. I thought those that believed the same as me would think that I was doing something wrong or sinful, and that was why God would not answer my prayers. My husband and I were struggling to hang on, ourselves. *Were we wrong? Had we heard God wrong? Were we only driven by our own desires and not God's will?*

> Trust in the Lord with all your heart and lean not on your own understanding; in all your ways submit to Him, and He will make your paths straight.
>
> —Proverbs 3:5-6 (NIV)

I could not figure it out, and I could not rationalize it in my mind.

The very next day, we went in for what is called a dilation and curettage (D&C), a procedure to remove tissue from inside the uterus. Interestingly enough, as I walked into the pre-op area, I saw another doctor that I worked with. *Oh, great, another person to witness my misery and see me in a hospital gown—ugh.*

The doctor came over to me and said, "I am so sorry; everything will be fine." He proceeded to kiss me on the top of my head, and honestly I felt like God himself was the one that comforted me at that moment through that elderly doctor.

My husband and our families were right there by my side and prayed the entire time.

> Even though I walk through the valley of the shadow of death, I will fear no evil, for you are with me; your rod and

your staff, they comfort me.

—Psalm 23:4 (BSB)

As you are reading this, if you are in a season of defeat, even in your darkest times, listen for God's voice. Take this time to find the light of Jesus in the Gospel. See and hear that God is with you.

> For I am convinced that neither death nor life, neither angels nor demons, neither the present nor the future, nor any powers, neither height nor depth, nor anything else in all creation, will be able to separate us from the love of God that is in Christ Jesus our Lord.
>
> —Romans 8:38-39 (NIV)

Not too long after the fourth miscarriage, we went to our church's annual couples' retreat. The destination was in Fort Caswell, North Carolina. It was a beautiful, quiet, and simple place. About seventy-five couples attended, and my husband and I were still wallowing in our spiritual and mental defeat. The first session of the retreat was an intimate experience of worship and dynamic speaking. Immediately after, I felt a strong urgency to publicly share our difficult journey to parenthood with the other couples at the retreat.

I told my husband about it, and he responded, "Are you sure we should do this?" We did not have a happy ending. God's scripture, "and they overcame by the blood of the Lamb, and by the word of their testimony..." came to my remembrance (see Revelation 12:11, NKJV).

Then I said, "Yes, we can do this!"

One of the hardest things we have ever done as a couple was get up in front of a room full of Christians and tell the story of what we viewed as a journey of defeat. However, the longer we spoke, the freer I felt in my spirit. I could feel that the Holy Spirit was giving me supernatural comfort, and He was building my faith even through what appeared in the natural as a defeat. After we spoke, there was not a dry eye in the room.

We ended our testimony by stating that we needed prayers to continue to build our faith for our miracle. We wanted to be parents, even if it meant I did not carry the baby myself.

There was what I would consider a spiritual mother of faith present during the marriage retreat. This woman of God prayed for me at the conclusion of that session. She prayed a specific, even graphic-sounding prayer over my body. She said words that included organs of my body and calling my body in line with what God has to say.

> ... you restored me to health and let me live. Surely it was for my benefit that I suffered such anguish. In your love, you kept me from the pit of destruction; you have put all my sins behind your back.
>
> —Isaiah 38:16-17 (NIV)

When she spoke these prayers and scriptures over me, I could physically feel the power from the Holy Spirit.

> For thus says the LORD: "Behold, I will extend peace to her like a river, and the glory of the nations like an overflowing stream; and you shall nurse, you shall be carried upon her hip, and bounced upon her knees."
>
> —Isaiah 66:12 (ESV)

Peace like a river—what a promise! The power was flooding my body with a peace that was weightless.

> "Come to me, all you who are weary and burdened, and I will give you rest. Take my yoke upon you and learn from me, for I am gentle and humble in heart, and you will find rest for your souls. For my yoke is easy and my burden is light."
>
> —Matthew 11:28-30 (NIV)

In that moment of prayer in a makeshift altar, I learned that it is important to pray specific prayers. God absolutely cares about the details of your life.

> The Lord directs the steps of the godly. He delights in every detail of their lives.
>
> —Psalm 37:23 (NLT)

I know to some I may sound extreme, but I want to pour into you that everything you will ever need is in His Word. Every scripture in the Bible is God-breathed, and it is meant to illuminate you as a person. The word becomes alive in your spirit, and your dreams and desires align with the will of God.

> When Jesus spoke again to the people he said, "I am the light of the world. Whoever follows me will never walk in darkness, but will have the light of life."
>
> —John 8:12 (NIV)

There may come a day in your own journey of faith, that you too, will need to share in the middle of the storm.

> "When you pass through the waters, I will be with you; and through the rivers, they shall not overwhelm you; when you walk through fire you shall not be burned, and the flame shall not consume you."
>
> —Isaiah 43:2 (ESV)

It takes faith to speak calm while still being in the storm. If we were able to expose our vulnerability with no evidence of healing, I have no doubt that you can too.

GUILT

The loss that we experienced in miscarriage brought out some hidden emotions not only in myself but also my husband. We both struggled with feeling guilty that in some way, we had caused the trauma that was now occurring in our lives. We analyzed our entire adulthood, starting from an age of accountability, and guilt would continue to flood our minds.

Guilt is a tactic that the enemy will use to hold your mind in captivity. Merriam-Webster states, guilt as a noun is defined as, "feelings of deserving blame especially for imagined offenses or from a sense of inadequacy." As a verb, Merriam-Webster defines guilt as, "to persuade (someone) to do something by causing feelings of guilt."[4]

Satan will use the emotion of guilt to try to persuade you that you are not good enough to receive God's grace and mercy. Do you know why Satan will use that strategy? It is because if he can delay you in any way shape or form from impacting the kingdom of God, then he will. He also is threatened by you as an active Christian. He is threatened by the difference you will make and the souls that you will go after for Christ. It is not you as a person; it is you as a witness. That is why it is even more important for you to know God's Word, so that you can use it to combat the mental games that Satan will try to play on your mind.

> In Him, we have redemption through His blood, the forgiveness of sins, according to the riches of His grace.
>
> —Ephesians 1:7 (NIV)

We have all sinned and fallen short of the glory of God, but God does not require us to be perfect. God knows that we will fail because we are human.

God desires for us to trust him and surrender our will to His. In the natural, my husband and I recognized that our situation appeared hopeless. We began to ask God for renewed hope and began praying prayers like the Lord's prayer.

> "Our Father, who art in heaven, hallowed be thy Name, thy kingdom come, thy will be done, on earth as it is in heaven. Give us this day our daily bread. And forgive us our trespasses, as we forgive those who trespass against us. And lead us not into temptation, but deliver us from evil. For thine is the kingdom, and the power, and the glory, for ever and ever. Amen."
>
> —Matthew 6:9-13 (KJV)

One Sunday morning at church, there was a set of newborn twins with an elderly woman sitting close to me during the service. During that service, she requested prayer for the babies because the mother of the babies had abandoned them and could not take care of them.

I had never seen these babies before. My spirit was drawn to these babies and this woman for this story. After the service, I approached her in the church parking lot to ask for more details about her situation. She proceeded to tell me that she was too old to take care of the newborns and knew the mom likely could not keep them and she was hoping they would not end up in an orphanage.

Something changed in my spirit that day. I felt like I came to a point in spiritual maturity that I had not reached prior to this moment. I prayed to God, "I surrender my will to yours to carry a baby." I want to be a mother, no matter how it happens. I expressed to the elderly woman my desire to adopt these twins if she agreed. She was thrilled to hear my confession and would contact me once they received a decision from the court system.

I believe God had been waiting for me to grow up spiritually and stop throwing a tantrum for what I wanted the way I wanted and just surrender to His plans for my life. He was molding me, shaping me, and He knew the desires of my heart because God designed me. He formed me in my mother's womb just as I hoped one day, He would form my offspring in my own womb. This all knowing and all powerful God even knows the number of hairs on my head, as well as yours.

A few weeks later, the elderly woman called me and told me that the court had ordered the children to be with their mother and the mother now wanted the babies back.

I was confused by this response, and I even questioned, "What in the world God?" I felt anger creep back in my thoughts at that moment. I will admit that I even felt like God was playing with my emotions like a yoyo. I knew I would have to hear from Him in a supernatural way in order to somehow face my current reality. *So here I am again God, guilty for my past, eager for the future, eager for promises to be fulfilled but left feeling confused at your plans for me.*

What does God's Word say about confusion?

If you are where I was in your walk with God, I would encourage you yet again not to get stuck in the feeling that you are experiencing, but always to take every emotion to the Word of God. His Gospel is the only source of true hope. In this world and in our human minds, we cannot comprehend the goodness of God nor His plans for us. In my life, I learned to not only trust in God, but also trust that God's process for the fulfillment of His plans would be just as beneficial to my maturity and growth as a Christian.

DISGUST

Comparison can be the thief of joy. I think most young adults would agree that it can be very discouraging to watch your newsfeed every day on social media. You may be comparing yourself to every individual's appearance, emotional description, wealth status depiction, or even worldly possessions. I think we all have to look at social media as a convenient way to keep in touch with others, but we also must realize that this is just their highlight reel. No one likes to post their struggles, insecurities, or defeats. Everyone loves to post the filtered pictures of themselves and their families. I know for myself, I may have to take ten pictures of our family to get one that I approve of to post on social media platforms.

It is easy to get lost in your interpretation of other's posts or pictures. Throughout my journey to parenthood, I became disgusted by what I read on social media. I would see posts about women who became pregnant and their birth stories during a time in my life that I was struggling and trying so hard to keep the faith. Deep down, I was envious of the successes of so many surrounding me. I needed to be reminded of what God has to say about envy because I grew a little more bitter every day.

> A tranquil heart gives life to the flesh, but envy makes the bones rot.
>
> —Proverbs 14:30 (ESV)

Every Mother's Day that passed, the more disgusted I became. It was just another reminder of the loss, grief, and emptiness I felt. God surely works in mysterious ways, but I felt like I could not see the light at the end of this tunnel.

A few months after my last miscarriage and failed attempt at adoption, I got a call from a mutual friend requesting that I take our church youth to a tent revival in a town close by so that they could do a drama at the service. I remember reaching out to a group of teenagers requesting them to come. I only heard back from one teenager.

Honestly, I didn't even want to go myself. It was a rainy, dreary day, and I was really annoyed that I had to go to another church service where I knew I would put another mask over my brokenness. I remember my stubborn attitude that night as I pulled up to this muddy field with a damp tent and a group of maybe fifty people.

My faithful teenager walked in obedience to God and did a musical drama to the anointed song, "Alabaster Box," by Cece Winans. The drama was great; it is a powerful song that speaks of a woman in the Bible who, although she had little, gave all of what she had and worshipped at the feet of Jesus. Even still, my rotten attitude wanted to leave, and I even thought about fleeing the scene. You see, I was burnt out on religion and services and longed for real wonder-working power as I had heard about from an older generation.

When the speaker got up to the pulpit, he began to talk, and I noticed there was another man standing with him at the pulpit. The speaker was preaching in another language, Spanish. I thought, *good grief God, how am I supposed to get anything out of this?* Here I am with, wet mud all over my shoes, it is pouring down raining by then, it stunk in that muggy tent, and I could not even understand the preacher without concentrating and listening to the interpreter. As you can tell, I was pretty ungrateful, and my spiritual maturity was dwindling fast.

I will never forget what happened next.

The preacher stopped preaching and said in broken English, "I must obey God." Everyone was frozen in silence. He said, "There is a woman here with a problem of the womb."

Umm, did I hear him correctly? I still sat there trying not to react, though my spirit was burning like fire on the inside.

He repeated, "There is a woman here with a problem of the womb—where are you? God is going to heal you tonight!" At that moment, I locked eyes with the preacher, and it seemed as if he was staring into my soul. He said, "Come here; it is you."

Tears streamed down my face; I began to repent of my bad attitude and sinful human nature. I prayed again, "Help me, God, with my unbelief."

The preacher said to me, "Not only will you have a child, but you will have children."

God must have a sense of humor. I cannot help but laugh at the fact that here I was, an ungrateful brat in the middle of a muddy field under a sweaty gnat-filled tent in a country rural town with a Hispanic minister, getting prophesied over. I was what some would call a hot mess, and God knew my flesh was becoming weak. Yet, still in all of His loving mercy, He ran after me. He spoke to me. He called me by name.

> But now, says the Lord— the one who created you, Jacob, the one who formed you, Israel: Don't fear, for I have redeemed you; I have called you by name; you are mine.
>
> —Isaiah 43:1 (ESV)

> For there is no respect of persons with God.
>
> —Romans 2:11 (KJV)

I was not worthy of that moment, but God loved me, and He loves you. If you are in a place of bitterness and disgust, and you feel like you are unworthy of God's miracles or goodness—think again. Take captive of that deceptive thought and fill your mind with God's Word. Proclaim God's Word and encourage yourself in the Lord; say if you did it for her, you can do it for me. God's Word is a covenant with His children. He is perfect and He does not lie.

I pray that you can find hope for your soul in reading about my imperfect walk with Christ and journey to be a light in my own personal darkness. I pray that you can feel the Father's embrace of love and comfort as I have when your situation looks hopeless or even disgusting in the natural. I pray that you will not let your emotional state paralyze your faith and ability to shine. No matter the outcome, God's Word is final. I seem to always go back to Jeremiah 29:11 (NIV),

> For I know the plans I have for you, plans to prosper you, not to harm you, to give you a hope and a future.

I spoke of happiness in a previous chapter, but happiness is based on circumstances and is temporary. It changes when the situation changes. Joy is from God.

> May the God of hope fill you with all joy and peace in believing, so that by the power of the Holy Spirit you may abound in hope.
>
> —Romans 15:13 (ESV)

Joy is a choice, an attitude of the heart and spirit. It is possible to feel joy during trials, it does not require a smile, and it can overlap with other emotions such as sadness, shame, and even anger. Happiness, on the other hand, cannot. Happiness is not present in your darkness. Joy will never leave during these times *if we choose it*. Joy can support our spirit regardless of our circumstances.

> Though you have not seen him, you love him. Though you do not now see him, you believe in him and rejoice with joy that is inexpressible and filled with glory.
>
> —1 Peter 1:8 (NIV)

My miracle had not yet come, but I could expect God to move, and I could be content knowing that I had experienced an undeniable encounter with Him. I can remember going to work the following Monday and sharing the tent revival story with my co-workers, and even their faith was encouraged. There was no physical evidence of the miracle, but our spirits knew the miracle was on the way.

ANTICIPATION

I had no idea how God's plan for me to have a child or children would happen as it had been prophesied in the last chapter. What was different now than all the other times before? The difference now in my faith was that while I was still eager to become a mother, I now had confidence in actually hearing the voice of God. I felt free to keep dreaming and hoping.

I remember going to a follow-up appointment at the last fertility specialist, and I saw a different doctor than before. Everything was different about this physician. He had no plans or answers—just compassion. He and I read articles of research of women who had multiple miscarriages and then successful pregnancies. This doctor simply said "I really do not understand, but I do think you can try again."

Six weeks later, I came to his office and had a positive pregnancy test confirmed by blood work and an ultrasound to prove a healthy baby! I will never forget spotting that heartbeat, beating strong, and the instant peace I felt in that moment.

Going forward, every single day, when we woke up, Allen would lay his hands on my stomach, and we would pray over this child. We prayed they would be intelligent, gifted, a genius even. We prayed that they would be healthy and whole in mind, body, and soul. Follow-up after follow-up and test after test continued to confirm our miracle. I realized that the longer I waited to become a mother in my suffering, the more impactful my testimony became of God's goodness and power.

My husband and I agreed to only share our miracle of pregnancy to close family and friends until we got through the first trimester. We felt that it was a wise decision. Even more amazingly, the end of my first trimester fell on Mother's Day in 2013.

I requested from my pastor at the time to share my testimony that day during church. Historically, the women in our church had started a tradition of wearing a hat if you were a mother. This memory is forever engrained in my mind. The excitement and anticipation in this moment was spoken with humility, genuine love, and compassion. There was not a dry eye in the sanctuary that day. At the end of my testimony, I reached down into a shopping bag that I had brought up to the stage with me. What joy erupted in that room as I pulled out a hat and placed it on my head. The atmosphere that day literally shifted, and you could feel it in a tangible way. The congregation was not only happy for my family and me, but they were encouraged that this was a miracle that God displayed through us. The same miracle that is also available to others. The Bible states,

> Ask and it will be given to you; seek and you will find; knock and the door will be opened to you.
>
> —Matthew 7:7 (NIV)

> This is the confidence we have in approaching God: that if we ask anything according to his will, he hears us. And if we know that he hears us—whatever we ask—we know that we have what we asked of him.
>
> —1 John 5:14-15 (NIV)

If you are reading this and you need a miracle, hang on. Never limit God; He is working even when we cannot see it. Sometimes the waiting is the preparation our hearts and minds need in order to appreciate the blessing that He is giving us.

How do you feel in most waiting rooms for any kind of appointment? Nervous? Eager? Impatient? At this point in my journey to motherhood, I began to struggle with my patience and my nervousness. Each appointment came and went, and I would secretly hold my breath before I heard that heartbeat or saw lab results. I had witnessed this amazing miracle, yet I still had trouble completely trusting Him to see it to fruition. I constantly had to renew my mind with God's Word.

> Do not conform to the pattern of this world, but be transformed by the renewing of your mind. Then you will be able to test and approve what God's will is—his good, pleasing, and perfect will.
>
> —Romans 12:2 (NIV)

Every month we were "that couple" that took a picture indicating the size of the baby and the month we made it to. Every month I would post my update, and people would see the visible evidence of God's power. So many women rejoiced with me because they knew the familiar feeling of infertility. The best month update to me was the month that the science books tell us the fetus is viable outside the womb, so just in case I went in preterm labor, the baby could survive. Looking back, I recognize that even that statement was still an indication that I was still struggling with some unbelief. God's Word says,

> And those who know your name put their trust in you, for you, O Lord, have not forsaken those who seek you.
>
> —Psalm 9:10 (NKJV)

We had one of those (popular at the time) gender reveal parties and cut into a cake to discover that this baby was a boy. We and our family and friends were so thrilled when we saw that blue cake frosting in-between the cake layers.

Do you remember earlier in this book when I told you that my husband and I gave our testimony in the middle of our journey without any sight of when victory would come? The next year at the couples' retreat, occurring in July, was only a few months away from our due date in November. When we all met in the meeting room, several people approached us in amazement because of my then very obvious pregnant belly. As I reflect on this time, I think—*wow, if we had not stood up in front of all those couples that year and shared the heartache of our journey, they would not be able to celebrate with us at that moment.*

I believe that sometimes we cannot really see the goodness of God in our lives until we can look in retrospect. Similarly, I believe that as time seems to go by slowly and we feel impatient for our promise, it is then that God is helping us live one step or day at a time. Maybe the reason is that He knows if we knew the whole story or had the entire list of directions to our destination, we may become overwhelmed and lost.

To illustrate this, think about how your map application on your phone will say the directions one step at a time. Can you imagine how overwhelmed you may feel if it said something like this? "Go one mile and turn left on this road and then go three miles and then turn right, go thirty-five miles on the highway, then go through the roundabout and make a sharp right turn, and you will be at your destination." I can imagine that I would be like, "What? I cannot remember what you said, can you repeat that? Wait! I don't think that is the best route, etc."

> The steps of a man are established by the Lord, when he delights in his way.
>
> —Psalm 37:23 (ESV)

It is wonderful to feel anticipation during a season of your life, but also take a moment to enjoy this journey that God has you on. Yes, enjoy it. The Bible also says,

> Consider it pure joy, my brothers and sisters, whenever you face trials of many kinds, because you know that

the testing of your faith produces perseverance. Let perseverance finish its work so that you may be mature and complete, not lacking anything.

—James 1:2-4 (NIV)

PAIN

Nine seemingly long months of labor anticipation would lead up to this memorable Sunday night. I was peacefully sleeping while dreaming I was physically feeling pain. I was confused until I woke up and realized that I was feeling contractions! I was excited but also a little scared because I did not know what these contractions would feel like. My excitement awakened my husband, and though he only had been asleep for about an hour, his adrenaline helped him pack the car and basically pace around in circles until I gave step-by-step instructions. We called our parents, close friends, and family even during the middle of the night. Talk about a fluctuation of emotions when you are having contractions. One minute you may be happy, the next scared, the next annoyed, and then next angry.

Hilariously, we made it to the hospital. To my surprise the nurse said that I was only one centimeter dilated, and I could either go home and come back later or I could stick around in the hospital during the remainder of the night and walk the halls to progress labor. I could not believe I was only one centimeter! The pain I was feeling was just the beginning of this childbirth experience—Thanks, Eve!

> To the woman He said: "I will greatly multiply your sorrow and your conception; in pain, you shall bring forth children."
>
> —Genesis 3:16 (NKJV)

Since we lived forty-five minutes from the hospital, we decided to stay and walk the halls. I remember doing jumping jacks in between contractions and walking around in my hot pink fuzzy robe. I guess I always have been a little "extra".

Soon enough, the contractions progressed and became more and more painful. The nurse checked on me again. This time she said, "Okay, we are going to admit you, and you are having a baby today!"

Yes, as we got the update we notified all our friends and family, and as hours passed by our waiting room volume grew steadily. So many generations of friends and family came to the hospital in anticipation of this child that we had all prayed for.

For this child I prayed; and the Lord hath given me my petition which I asked of him.

—1 Samuel 1:27 (KJV)

My pain increased naturally as childbirth is designed. I was advised to get an epidural to help with the pain. The epidural was only somewhat effective for the pain. After several hours of labor, in fact twenty hours later, there was a moment of panic during the pain. The nurse began shaking my big pregnant belly with a ghost white appearance on her face. "What is wrong?" I asked. The nurse stated that the baby had a complication, and his heart rate dropped for several minutes. Scared, we all began to pray and it seemed as though time was standing still. Surely God would not get us this far in the journey for us to lose this precious child we prayed for. The heartbeat finally came back up, and the medical team came in and advised a C-section (cesarean delivery). No time for more pain medication or mental preparation, tears streamed down my cheeks.

I can remember my mom saying to me, "Do not worry, everything will be fine, you will not be any less of a mother because of the way the baby is delivered." She had that strange discernment that only a mother has and knew without me even saying it that I was scared. They rushed me to the operating room. The doctor said there was no time to wait and began to cut me open. My epidural at that time had completely worn off, but there was no time to replace it with different anesthesia. I can remember every agonizing moment of what seemed to last an eternity as I told my doctor four times, I felt the cutting. I was in so much pain my body trembled and tears rolled down my face.

It was so worth it, though!

What actually was only a few seconds of agony brought forth this absolutely beautiful red-headed, blue-eyed, and healthy baby boy. According to our families, the waiting room erupted with joy and shouts of praise for the miracle that everyone had prayed for. What an amazing testimony of the healing power and faithfulness of our good, good Father. His grace is sufficient for you as well.

Maybe you are reading this and you are in pain maybe physically or mentally. Maybe you think that you are too far gone, "backslid" that is, or maybe you have never known God or had a relationship with him. No man is perfect. God's Word says,

> For all have sinned and fall short of the glory of God.
>
> —Romans 3:23 (NIV)

Be encouraged because if you are starved for the supernatural love of a Father and Friend, God is here. He has always been there. His Word says that,

> My flesh and my heart may fail, but God is the strength of my heart and my portion forever.
>
> —Psalm 73:26 (NIV)

Some questioned our endurance throughout this process of becoming parents, and all we could say is that we have witnessed the power of God. There is no way we can deny His presence or greatness. God's Word says,

> "I have told you these things, so that in me you may have peace. In this world you will have trouble. But take heart! I have overcome the world."
>
> —John 16:33 (NIV)

I also am reminded that although pain is described as subjective to the individual, the worst pain in history was experienced from the son of God who died on the cross, a gruesome, horrific death just so that God could spend eternity with us. John 3:16 (NIV) says,

For God so loved the world that he gave his one and only Son, that whoever believes in him shall not perish but have eternal life.

He loved you and me that much. I will spend the rest of my days honoring the God who saved me, healed me, and filled me with hope.

TIRED

We named our miracle baby boy Hudson Jude, Hudson means "river" and Jude means "praise".

> "Whoever believes in me, as the Scripture has said, 'Out of his heart will flow rivers of living water.'"
>
> —John 7:38 (NIV)

Hudson was our river of praise, a constant reminder of the promises of God.

I am sure that any parent of a newborn would describe their most common feeling throughout the first year of the infant's life as tired—maybe even exhausted. I can attest to that.

Our pediatrician at that time told us that we had a newborn at the highest risk time of the year. November, historically for our region, has been a peak of flu season. The doctor advised me to only take our son to the doctor for check-ups, but not to take him out and about for at least eight weeks so that he could stay well. Being the new mom "first timer" I followed the doctor's advice religiously. Hudson did not sleep well, he cried a lot, and after my husband's week off for paternity leave, I grew lonely. I can remember crying every day when Allen would leave for work and I cried when the sun went down because I knew it would be a long night of rocking. I was ashamed of how I felt because, after all, God answered my prayers for this newborn, and at the least I felt I should not complain.

As I reflect on my emotional state at that time, I see a woman who was exhausted, trying to heal physically, still grieving, and trying to find joy in the midst of a completely different atmosphere. All I knew to do was to seek to hear God's voice by reading His Word. I found this verse,

> My grace is sufficient for you, for my power is made perfect in weakness. Therefore I will boast all the more gladly of my weaknesses, so that the power of Christ may rest upon me. For the sake of Christ, then, I am content with weaknesses, insults, hardships, persecutions, and calamities. For when I am weak, then I am strong.
>
> —2 Corinthians 12:9 (NKJV)

Our most vulnerable moments are when God can mold and shape us the most. Do not be ashamed of your weaknesses. God created you, and He knows you more than anyone and He is the only one who can pull you up and out of the pit you may feel like you are in. Knowing your identity in Christ is so important. You are a daughter of the King—yes, you have royal blood the day you accepted Jesus Christ as your Lord and Savior.

> Therefore, there is now no condemnation for those who are in Christ Jesus.
>
> —Romans 8:1 (NIV)

My spirit was not being fed by a Sunday or Wednesday night service like I was in the past. This was seven years ago so streaming online services was not really a trend yet. My soul was thirsty for replenishment. If you are that soul hungry person reading this right now, open your Bible and let God speak to you.

I would hate that my husband would get to go to church and I could not. I was trying my best to breastfeed my child and felt so confined, yet happy, because I was the only one who could feed him. Sometimes we are so busy as women, trying to take care of our families, cooking, feeding, cleaning, and the list goes on and on, that we neglect our spiritual needs.

I can remember a time when I thought, *today is going to be a productive day.* I refused to be in my pajamas with dried up crusted milk and matted up hair when Allen came home from work. What motivation I started with. Shortly after a successful feeding session, I laid down my son in his cradle and hurried quietly to get a shower, likely my first in five days. The moment I got the shampoo good and lathered up, I heard screaming crying coming from the nursery. Scared because I was the only one home, I went running down the hall drenched and soap lathered up in my hair and now sopping wet footprints in the carpet just to find Hudson completely fine, just crying. *Well just forget it! I am just going to sit here and rock this baby all day.*

Isn't that so typical that when we have a plan and are feeling so motivated that one little bump in the road can cause us to give up?

I can remember crying out to God and asking Him to help me to be the best mother and wife and honor Him with my life. What was interesting was that even though I grieved being in the company of believers and getting fed by preachers, speakers, and stage worship, I knew God blessed me through this season. When I cried out to God, He always came to the rescue.

If you look at the scriptures that tell of impactful encounters with Jesus and women, you will find that He always came to them. He came to the tormented woman at the well who was forgiven, the dying mother-in-law of a disciple who was healed, the woman who touched the hem of his garment and was healed, and the woman He called over who was known to be crippled for eighteen years and was healed. Jesus allowed women that were at his tomb to be the first to see His resurrection. God's Word is full of moments where He came to them, He brought healing to them. He knew they had domestic responsibilities, so He came to them. His presence comes to us today.

Women of God, do not be discouraged in your surrounding environment because His Holy Spirit dwells inside of you. He can restore you suddenly with His power because He loves you. Second Peter 1:3 (ESV) says,

> His divine power has granted to us all things that pertain to life and godliness, through the knowledge of him who called us to his own glory and excellence.

God made you a woman because He has a special mission for you. Women are strong yet caring, stern yet gentle, and tough yet loving. Women are resilient with God's power and strength. The world today needs Godly women full of faith and full of God's Word. God is calling Gospel-filled women to shine in the darkness and even get messy. The unreached harvest oftentimes won't be in our crisp clean churches, they will be in the trenches.

Just like glitter creates an endless mess as it spills from it's container, your light should overflow and get everywhere. The more glitter spreads, the harder it is to wipe out. Keep learning to shine the love of Christ in the darkness. You may not feel qualified for the assignment God has given you, but believe me, if He chose you for it, you will be equipped... as long as you learn to stay connected with your source, the Father's Word.

NEEDY

About six weeks after our miracle baby boy was born, I noticed that Hudson was fussy after feedings. He even appeared to be in discomfort after feedings. I said earlier that he cried a lot, and by a lot, I mean all the time. I did not have a previous baby to recognize or know that anything was wrong.

I mentioned it to our pediatrician at his wellness appointment, and the doctor told me that he thought Hudson had a milk protein allergy to my breastmilk. He found that there was actually microscopic blood in Hudson's stool, likely causing his extreme discomfort. I could not believe that my breast milk was causing him so much discomfort!

My doctor advised that we start a milk formula rather than breastmilk due to his findings. *Okay, I do not know how we can make room in our already tight budget for formula, but surely it will not cost too much.* He then proceeded to tell me that the type of formula Hudson needed was the most expensive on the market at that time because he had to have the purest form for digestion.

My mom was with me at the appointment, and she was always reassuring me and trying to comfort me. The doctor said he would give me a few samples to start with, and he told me where I could purchase the formula. I can remember breaking down crying all the way home from the doctor's office. Online, I found out the formula costs forty-four dollars a can. A single can, not a case—a can. That can would not last more than a couple of days. I knew there was no way we could afford that formula.

My husband and I, looking back, may not have made the wisest decisions financially. We both worked full time and had decent jobs, but right after we got married, we bought a new house that was too big for two adults and two brand new vehicles. Our tithe, a large house payment, two car payments, utility bills, food expenses, and the list went on, would leave no room in our tight budget for costly formula.

My mother just continued to tell me everything would be okay. She said, "Let's go have a good lunch. I will pay, and maybe it will help you take your mind off of this curveball."

Okay, I thought. We had not been to this fairly popular steak house before, and it was the middle of a weekday. *Surely it would not be packed with people and safe to take the baby.*

We get there, and it is this super fancy restaurant with dim lighting and an a la carte expensive menu. All of a sudden, Hudson started crying, whaling even. I searched for the restroom because by then, I was getting the stink-eye from the other customers and waiters. There was no nursing station in the restroom, not even a chair. I had not brought any bottles or nursery water to fill with my new formula, so I would have to breastfeed him in this restroom. I can remember sitting on a toilet in a tiny stall trying to feed a screaming baby and change a messy diaper. By this point, my nerves were shot and my mom was texting me saying, "What do you want me to order for you?" I finally got Hudson calmed down enough to go back to the table, I thought, and by then my mom had gotten her beverage and the complimentary bread basket. Hudson suddenly started crying again! I told mom we had to leave.

What a sight we were. A frazzled new mom with breastmilk likely all over my shirt, sweat beading off my face from struggling to nurse on a toilet, and smeared mascara from all the earlier tears. I knew Hudson was in discomfort and that we would have to leave. We told our waiter what was going on (as if he couldn't tell himself) and we apologetically left. *Is this what it will always be like?* We left and found a drive thru at a fast-food restaurant on the way home.

My dilemma was still at the forefront of my thoughts. *How would we afford this expensive formula?* I applied for assistance for the formula, but because my husband and I both had full-time jobs we did not qualify for any assistance. I bought a case consisting of four cans online, and the price was around one hundred and fifty dollars. I knew this would run out fast, and I needed provision. The formula did seem to help our son. The crying improved, he started sleeping better, and he just seemed more content. To me, that was a miracle in itself. Still though, now I know we have to have the formula, but still had no idea how we could pay for it without running up credit card debt.

I can specifically remember as I pulled out the last can of formula from the kitchen cabinet, I teared up and said to myself, "God, I need help." Immediately it was as if time stood still as I remembered the story of the widow and the prophet Elijah. He told her to bring him a loaf of bread, and she told him that she did not have enough for him, only for herself and her son. Elijah persisted and stated that God said He would supply.

> Elijah said to her, "Don't be afraid. Go home and do as you have said. But first, make a small loaf of bread for me from what you have and bring it to me, and then make something for yourself and your son. For this is what the Lord, the God of Israel, says: 'The jar of flour will not be used up and the jug of oil will not run dry until the day the Lord sends rain on the land." She went away and did as Elijah had told her. So, there was food every day for Elijah, and for the woman and her family. For the jar of flour was not used up and the jug of oil did not run dry, in keeping with the word of the Lord spoken by Elijah.
>
> —1 Kings 17:13-16 (NIV)

This is why it is important to hide the Word of God in your heart. That day I told God, if you can do it for her, you can do it for me. I will stand on your promise because you are Jehovah Jireh, my provider.

I began to send out text messages to people I knew who worked in pediatric offices asking for samples of this expensive formula. One nurse that I knew only by mutual acquaintances was able to provide me with some formula. Then word got out, and people began texting me with offers of formula samples. My work manager had a neighbor who did not know me at all and gave me twelve cases of formula. I was completely overwhelmed at the generosity of these random people. I recognized though that they were not random at all; they were divinely appointed to meet my needs. God heard my cry and He provided the need. I never bought another case or can of formula after all our donated cans. Cling to God's Word and declare it over your needs and situation.

...bring the full tithe into the storehouse, that there may be food in my house. And thereby put me to the test, says the Lord of hosts, if I will not open the windows of heaven for you and pour down for you a blessing until there is no more need.

—Malachi 3:10 (ESV)

If you have a need right now, tithe. First reason being, that is already God's. Secondly, obedience is important to God.

Every tithe of the land, whether of the seed of the land or of the fruit of the trees, is the Lord's; it is holy to the Lord.

—Leviticus 27:30 (ESV)

God will be faithful to His Word. If He can do it for us, He can surely do it for you. God's favor is available to all of His children. Do not be ashamed of your neediness. The dependency on God and the fulfillment of these promises are a demonstration of God's power that someone else needs to see through you.

Thank you, God, for answering our prayers of need as we come before you. We know you will not withhold any good thing from your children. God, help us to trust in your plans for our lives.

CONTENT

Time passed after we saw the miracle of provision in our home, and now God was really showing off. According to our pediatrician, occasionally children can outgrow some of these cow protein allergies. He said that if I continued to pump and save breastmilk, we might be able to use it again.

I thought that seemed like a great idea, and I chose to believe that Hudson would improve and heal and that he would be able to use breast milk. About nine months later, we began to reintroduce breast milk in a bottle, and he seemed not to have any issues. Almost exactly at one-year-old, Hudson was able to go through all my stored up frozen milk. In one year, we could start introducing regular whole milk. I know this may be too much detail for some, but to have as severe an allergy as our son had, it was a miracle that he was able to tolerate my stockpiled breast milk.

Hudson seemed to develop normally from that moment on. He started walking, talking, and we were just overjoyed and content in the enjoyment of this family that God blessed us with. My mom was able to retire from a twenty-five year career in healthcare and keep our son so that we would not have added cost of a daycare facility, and we could both continue to work full time. All was right in our world.

Early in 2015, I noticed I didn't quite feel normal; I had some nausea and just felt different. I thought it might be a good idea to see my doctor. Interestingly enough, they gave me a pregnancy test, and to my shock and surprise it was positive. We were surprised because we did not think it would be easy for us to have another child after our previous experiences with frequent miscarriage. I was worried because I did not want to have another miscarriage.

The doctors ran all the lab work and did an ultrasound, and this was another healthy pregnancy—no issues at all. God was blessing us again. I will not lie and say I was not a little bit anxious considering we had a young toddler at home. My lab results continued to be within normal limits, and the new baby number two seemed to be developing normally. We were blessed beyond measure.

One hot day in July, while we were both working, my mom called and said that Hudson was crying uncontrollably and she did not know what was wrong. She said he was telling her he was hurting. I immediately left work and met her at the pediatrician's office. The doctor said they could not guarantee that something harmful was not going on in his intestines and that they would like for him to go to the emergency room to get a thorough work-up. This was traumatic to all of us.

Me (pregnant, hormonal, and emotional), Allen, and my mom headed to the local children's emergency room. Hudson is crying still, and the medical staff are trying to draw blood and do other tests. This was a very difficult hospital visit.

I can remember laying with Hudson on the stretcher, praying over him and singing "Jesus Loves You" and "Jesus Loves the Little Children" to try and comfort him. They gave him pain medication through an intravenous line and it seemed to ease his pain. They ran all kinds of tests and they never found out what was wrong.

My husband and I were supposed to be volunteering at vacation Bible school at our church that night. As we waited in the emergency room, we were messaging our church family and requesting prayers over our son. He seemed to improve, so the doctors were at a loss of a diagnosis and sent us home. Hudson continued to do well and did not seem to have any more pain. Praise God for touching our son's body and that the doctors had no explanation of the symptoms.

Looking back, I noticed something seemed to change with Hudson and his personality. He started getting quiet. He was not talking as much as he had been prior. We wondered what was going on. *What could cause this? Maybe we were just overthinking this and needed just to relax.* Some time would pass, but I can remember going on vacation that summer being on the edge the whole time, wanting Hudson to snap back into his normal self.

I was waiting to feel some kind of peace by hearing Hudson use his words to communicate. It had been a long time since we had heard Hudson say, "I love you." One day while we were at the beach, he was watching one of his favorite shows on television and out of the blue he said, "I love you." It appeared as if he was telling the mice characters on the television show that he loved them. *How can he tell them he loves them and he hasn't said that to me in forever? At least he spoke, though.* I remember feeling like I was wearing a mask of contentment in public at this point, but underneath the mask was worry and fear about Hudson's regression in speech.

It is important to note that we are all guilty of wearing masks in our day to day lives. The mask of strength seems to be of much desire to many, including myself, especially during difficult seasons. The mask of happiness seems to be a great disguise, according to most social media posts. Even the mask of a victim is desired by some so that there is an excuse or explanation of their constant need for attention. The myriad display of masks that we wear daily may fool some people, but they cannot fool God. He knows the truth. He has known us since the day He formed us in our mother's wombs.

The raw, real, and exposed me may be undesirable, to say the least. I think that is a lot of my purpose in writing this book. I can remember growing up around all kinds of seemingly strong Christian women. I can remember feeling insecure because I saw only the outside of their faith and thought they were so much better than me. *I must be weak*, I thought, *to feel as deeply as I felt.* I hid my emotions in times where I shouldn't in an effort to appear strong. I struggled with emotions during times and trials of my life. I believe that there is a young generation of women who need to hear the stories, the real, the raw, and exposed stories of the older generations in order to survive. There is an impartation that must take place between an older generation and a younger generation. The anointing and wisdom to be gained are priceless. The greatest mentors in my own life were those that let their guards down and shared testimonies of

God's faithfulness in their own lives.

We cannot continue to hide or wallow in our emotions; we must go to God's Word and testimonies of truth to be encouraged. Our lives are already out there for criticism because of social media, smartphones, and technology advances. The rate of people comparing and envying each other's lives continues to rise. God designed us as emotional beings for a reason, but the only way we can be overcomers is by the word of our testimony. God's plan for your life is to impact the world with the light of His son.

When you ask for forgiveness of your sins and ask Jesus into your heart, you also receive His Holy Spirit. His Spirit lives in you; you are marked by the Holy Spirit. It is no longer enough to get saved and never do anything else. The darkness of the world that we are living in needs your light. There may come a day that you cannot find or read a Bible. Make sure you get it in your heart and mind so that you can know what God's promises for your life are. The same blessing that God promised to the seed of Abraham is for you. Take the mask off and let God mold and shape you and let someone around you witness the miracles and goodness of God in you.

CONFUSED

The rollercoaster of my emotions would leave me confused as I analyzed my son's symptoms and changes in behavior. One day I would be worrying over Hudson's regression of speech, and then I would see a glimpse of normalcy, and I would calm down. I was so confused about his patterns of behavior. I remember going to his eighteen-month-old well-child check-up and expressing my concerns to our pediatrician, the same pediatrician we had when Hudson was born. The doctor did not seem alarmed at Hudson's speech; he thought that maybe some of it may be emotional since he might be realizing that he will be gaining a sibling. I was okay with that answer, but I still had this gnawing feeling in my gut that something did not seem right.

In August of 2015, Hudson became a big brother to a beautiful baby sister. She was a scheduled smooth delivery, unlike her brother's emergency delivery. This birth experience was not a traumatic encounter. We named her Charlotte Rose because she was so beautiful, and Charlotte is the female version of Charles which was my grandfather, or "pappy's" name. Charlotte in Hebrew means free man. She would be our free spirit.

The day Charlotte was born, I had this picture in my head of how this was supposed to go. My family would bring Hudson to the hospital to meet his new baby sister. He would be so happy to meet her, love to kiss her maybe, and smile big for a picture of this perfect appearing family.

This is not the way it happened.

Hudson walked into the room and ran to my bedside with a smile on his face and wanted for me to pick him up, only to realize there was this baby in my arms. He immediately started crying uncontrollably, to the point he cried himself to sleep in my husband's lap.

What in the world is going on? I even thought I was the worst mom ever, and I must have handled that situation all wrong. I analyzed every moment of that encounter and how I could perhaps fix this. The facts were that I could not fix anything and that God was the only one who could. When we came home from the hospital, Hudson's tolerance to his new baby sister improved, but it seemed he still was quickly regressing verbally. Charlotte, on the other hand, was a dream of a baby. God knew what I would and would not be able to handle. She was the baby that breastfed well, slept well, and was content.

During this season and while I was still on maternity leave from work, I felt this sensing in my spirit out of nowhere that I needed to change jobs. My mom was still going to be my primary childcare, but I still felt that my season at my current job was ending.

I loved my job. I had worked at my job for close to eight years at this point, and my coworkers were my second family. I met and learned from some of who I believe are the greatest nurses. I was comfortable at my job, I felt that I was self-sufficient in my role, and I liked being an experienced nurse in my department. I had completed every leadership ladder course that I could, and I felt I was on the way to advancement within that organization. My desires career-wise were all centered around the dream that I would be a leader in some form or fashion in the nursing field one day. Still though, that nagging feeling did not go away.

I was so confused as to why God would place this desire in my spirit when in my heart I wanted to advance within my own organization. I was also confused because my hormones were all over the place. I was worried about Hudson, and I did not know how my mom would be able to handle a newborn and a toddler that required a lot of one-on-one attention.

I went to God's Word and found Scripture that would help me remember that I can ask God to give me understanding, such as this verse:

Think over what I say, for the Lord will give you

understanding in everything.

—2 Timothy 2:7 (ESV)

One day while sitting in Charlotte's nursery rocking her, I decided just to look and see what opportunities were out there in my job field. I happened to see a job posting for a staff nurse position at a local clinic in my hometown. This would be a lot closer to home for me, and it was newly owned by the same organization that my current workplace was under. Historically, this potential new employer did not have the best reputation in town, but it would be under completely new leadership. I decided to take a leap of faith and put my resume out there.

It was only a few days later when I got a call from the office manager. I was asked to come in for an interview. The interview went well, but I will never forget that the manager asked me some hard questions. She said, "You seem to be a nurse who has done a lot of courses, and it seems as though you may be desiring to climb a career ladder." She proceeded to tell me that she did not want to give me any false hope because this role was only for a staff nurse position. She asked would I be satisfied in a staff nurse position because that was all they had to offer.

I explained that I felt that God was telling me to be obedient to His calling and that I needed to do this to be closer to my family. A perk was that this workplace was only five miles down the road from my parents. I felt that I could put my career desires on hold in order to be the best mom I could. I interviewed with the physician later as well, and he wanted to meet my whole family (which at the time I thought was rather strange to be honest), but then again this was a completely different setting than where I had previously worked.

The interview went well. I went home and prayed about it all and had my family praying as well. I can remember praying for provision as well because this job would be a more lateral move and likely a pay cut. It just so happened that, simultaneously, my husband and I were on the way to look at a bigger vehicle since we now had two huge car seats to climb over every day. On the way to the car lot, we held hands and prayed together and asked God that if it was His will for me to take this job that they would offer me an "x" dollar amount.

While we were driving, we got a call from the human resource department offering me the job, and they offered the exact amount we prayed for! We could not believe it. Now we felt God had confirmed it and sealed the deal. Even after feeling so sure of this plan, I still had to convince myself because this would be a whole different nursing field, different specialty, and I would be in a place where I knew no one.

I wrestled with the decision and still felt confused, so I knew I needed to hear what God had to say. I knew that God's Word said that He was not the author of confusion. I searched for answers in God's Word, and I found these verses,

> ...thus says the Lord, your Redeemer, the Holy One of Israel: "I am the Lord your God, who teaches you to profit, who leads you in the way you should go."
>
> —Isaiah 48:17 (NASB)

> ...the heart of man plans his way, but the Lord establishes his steps.
>
> —Proverbs 16:9 (ESV)

Okay, so now I began to feel more confident in what my decision would be. By this time, my maternity leave was ending, and I would need to return to my current job to give my notice instantly.

I was best friends with my clinical coordinator, and we all felt like a close family there. This would be the hardest decision I would have to make at that point in my career. It was a blind faith move in a lot of ways because I knew this would not be an easy transition. I would have to trust that even though it did not feel good in the natural sense that it was the right move in the supernatural.

In Biblical history, it is apparent that God's plans rarely are sensible. If you read the Bible, you will see where he told people to do seemingly crazy tasks out of obedience, but He would bless them later. Just look at Abraham and Isaac's story in the very first book of the Bible, Genesis chapter twenty-two. Here is a father of what was promised many generations as many as the stars even, and God tells Abraham to take his promised son up a mountain and sacrifice him to God. Sacrifice his miracle son? Can you imagine what Abraham was thinking? As a parent, I know that had to be the hardest task, and I likely would have been disobedient had I been in Abraham's shoes. Abraham remembered and trusted God's promises not only for the miracle of a son but that he would be a father to many generations. I often think that Abraham had already seen God provide a miracle against human odds by impregnating his elderly wife, Sarah. Maybe every moment in our own walks of life as we are obedient to the leading of His Holy Spirit, God is continually stretching our faith. Abraham did as God told him, but when he got to the top of the mountain God stopped Abraham. The message was, "Now I know you fear God." God provided an alternate sacrifice, a ram. What a relief I would imagine it was, to not only Abraham but, I am sure, Isaac was even more relieved. I would imagine as Isaac was bound to that altar that he was so confused and scared, but now he could trust his father and his heavenly father. Maybe if we will remember the promise like Abraham did all those years ago, then we can begin to trust him with our future and our generations to come.

In my own life at the time, I was still learning to trust God's plans. I returned to my current workplace with this aching news that I would have to leave after just returning from maternity leave. I was sad, they were sad, we were all sad, but they knew that my faith in God was so important to me. They had witnessed first-hand the miraculous pregnancies of not only one child but two children. They were the ones sometimes that held me up when I felt like falling down. Most everyone was supportive of my decision and wished me the best.

While I was working out the last week of my notice, I suddenly had sharp pains in my side. The pain gripped me and I had to lay on the floor in the hallway because the pain was so severe. My best friend took me across the street to the emergency room. Shortly after an assessment, they told me I would need to have my gallbladder taken out. The doctors also stated that apparently, this was very common after childbirth in women. I was confused then too because I could not understand why I would have to leave my job with a bang by having a surgery and then having to start a new job right after surgery. Nothing seemed to make sense in my life at the time, but I had already decided to leave so I had my surgery and recovered as quickly as possible in order to start my new job.

Charlotte, who had been a dream of a newborn, was now having a very hard time with feedings and sleeping right after my surgery because I had to rely on family members to take care of her for a few days. Talk about an emotional rollercoaster. My whole purpose in describing all of this journey is that you may be at a crossroads of needing to make a decision that does not seem to make sense, but you know God is leading you. Take the step of faith; God will make the way. You may not understand now, but maybe you will someday. His plans are always better than ours. The confusion of the now cannot compare to the peace of walking in obedience in the future.

> For my thoughts are not your thoughts, neither are your ways my ways declares the Lord. As the heavens are higher than the earth, so are my ways higher than your ways and my thoughts than your thoughts.
>
> —Isaiah 55:8-9 (NIV)

OVERWHELMED

In December of 2015, I started my new job. I was still recovering from gallbladder surgery, I had two children at home, I was up all hours of the night for feedings, I was still worried about my son's speech, and I was trying to learn a completely different specialty of nursing. To say I was feeling overwhelmed is likely an understatement.

Looking back, I know it was only by the grace of God that I was able to get through that season. One weekend, I could tell I was wearing extremely thin and feeling like I was about to have an emotional meltdown. I can even remember searching for a psychiatrist or therapist because I felt so overwhelmed and alone in my thoughts and emotions. I am not ashamed to say that I went and spoke with a professional. At the time, I thought that I might have just an attention problem, and maybe I just could not focus because I had an attention-deficit disorder. Actually, the professional thought more than anything I was overwhelmed and hyper-anxious. She said I was fearful of what may come because of what I had gone through. She told me she felt I was overwhelmed and exhausted emotionally because my brain was working overtime, trying to problem-solve and figure out everything.

Life was so busy, and I felt like I was a spinning top on the floor about to fall down. At that moment, I knew that I needed to take captive of all anxious thoughts that were holding my mind in bondage, but I really did not know how. I told my husband that I had to find an outlet. I was missing church a lot because of small children and needed encouragement. I really needed some Godly women in my life.

The very next Sunday, I walked into church and a greeter handed me a piece of paper stating that they were launching a women's Bible study that would meet once a week. *Wow, God really did come to the rescue.* Our church had not had a women's ministry of any kind in years, and at my breaking point a women's Bible study was birthed. I remember being like, "Sign me up!"

My husband was in total agreement because he knew I needed to climb out of the emotional pit that I was in. I also needed to learn from women who were spiritually stronger and wiser than I was. My mind, soul, and spirit needed to mature.

At the first Bible study meeting I went to, I was the youngest woman there, but I immediately felt at home. The study the leader had chosen was *Breaking Free* by Beth Moore. This study was published in 1999, but it could not have been more relevant to now. I needed to study and learn and realize what true freedom in Christ was. I had to break free from the bondage of fear and anxiety that gripped my mind and thought-life long enough. I knew I was not yet equipped for all that God was calling me to. Weeks went by, and the lessons and knowledge I gained not only from the study but also from the other women's testimonies in our group were life changing. The relationships that I developed with other women became as close as family.

The state of mind that I was in prior to the Bible study would never be able to absorb the knowledge and experience that I would need to begin my new job. I became extremely reliant on God in my new role because I literally knew no one at my new job, and it was a small office. Instead of loud break room lunch talks packed with co-workers like I was used to, it was a lot of eating by myself and reading or praying to God.

> I lift up my eyes to the mountains where does my help come from? My help comes from the Lord, the Maker of heaven and earth. He will not let your foot slip, he who watches over you will not slumber; indeed, he who watches over Israel will neither slumber nor sleep.
>
> —Psalm 121:1-4 (NIV)

God knew I would need his strength and comfort as I faced this season, so He pulled me out of a place of comfort and guided me where I would be close to Him.

So much of my world was changing and changing fast. My husband

and I still had a lot of concerns over Hudson's speech development and made an appointment with his pediatrician to discuss. Things had not improved with time, as we had hoped before. The doctor made a referral for Hudson to receive an evaluation by the state's children's development agency. They had speech therapists, physical therapists, and psychologists and would be able to bring light to what was going on. I was terrified at what they might say. I knew just from being a nurse that the symptoms pointed to a developmental delay or disorder along the lines of autism, but I refused to accept it.

We went to the first appointment with a speech therapist, and the evaluation was awful. The room was tiny and packed with my mother, husband, son, and I. Our two year old was hysterical and had zero interest in participating in this assessment. It was boiling hot in the room, I was almost in tears myself and desperately pleading with Hudson to cooperate. It was a disaster. At the end of this nightmare of a visit, the speech therapist said that she was concerned and saw several red flags that pointed to a diagnosis of autism. She said she could not ultimately diagnose him with autism because she was not a physician, but she was concerned and recommended further evaluation.

We left the speech therapy evaluation devastated. *How could this be good for Hudson? How could this happen to our miracle baby boy? Would we ever hear his voice again? Why is God allowing this to happen to him, to us?* I can remember going to work the next day, and several people asked me about our appointment and I just busted out crying.

If you know anything about autism spectrum disorder, it can be a broad spectrum of mild symptoms to severe. Some children are permanently disabled, and some improve with early intervention. We had no idea what we were facing. We had to go through the motions of searching for the best doctor to provide an official diagnosis.

I was in so much denial personally that I thought that maybe if we just ignored this, it would improve and it would get better. That did not help the situation at all. I knew here is another moment in our lives where we would have to rely on God for strength and direction. Evaluation after evaluation all confirmed in the doctor's eyes that Hudson was indeed diagnosed with autism. I know that there are a lot worse diagnoses than autism, but as a mother and as parents you never want your child to struggle.

The word "autism" comes from the Greek word "autos," which means "self." It describes conditions in which a person is removed from social interaction. In other words, he becomes an "isolated self." My interpretation of this definition is "alone." This broke my heart for him. We had to get help, and we had to get it now.

Eventually, we were able to get Hudson into some speech therapy and into the public-school preschool program. Hudson cried every day when my mom took him to school. He seemed to hate it. I was so completely anxious that I constantly emailed his teacher requesting updates on his behavior. Yes, I was that annoying mother I am sure, but I was scared of this new system, new environment, new diagnosis, and a new way of life. We were learning how to navigate this while also trying to cling to God's Word and not label our child, but to be an overcomer of this label.

For the life of me I could not see how this should be a part of God's plan for Hudson. I was honestly angry, sad, grieved, and felt like God went silent on me. *How can I function with all of this emotional turmoil inside?*

Several months passed, and all the while, I am looking and reading research articles of treatment plans, better doctors, better therapists, better schools, and even better prayers that I can pray. I believe I was silently hoping I would help God heal Hudson so he would not have to struggle to communicate or fit in. I felt such a loss of control and literally felt like I was spinning in a cyclone of uncertainty of the future.

Allen and I began to feel captive to our home because we did not want to have ugly looks or stares from people as to why our two year old still drank milk from a bottle or why he is not talking or why the only way we can go out is to let him be distracted with a movie on our phones. More than our feelings, we did not know how much Hudson understood because of his verbal limitations so we did not want his feelings hurt. That seems to be a common trait of most parents, right? We want to protect them from the world and shield them so they will not have their feelings hurt. It was so bad that we lost friends and close fellowship with friends because we were so limited by schedules and outbursts of behaviors. We isolated our family from most special occasions in fear of what others would think and to protect Hudson.

One day we were sitting at home tormented by our isolation that we decided that we could no longer live in fear. If Hudson has an outburst, oh well; if he needs to drink a milk bottle, oh well; if he pees in his pants at the table, oh well. That feisty momma bear attitude rose up in me that I would stand up to any bullies that had something to say. We decided to go eat at a local Mexican restaurant, and it was the best decision ever. It was loud enough in the restaurant that no one cared if he cried or if our younger child, Charlotte, cried. He loved the instant gratification of chips at the table so he did not have to wait. We also were able to withhold him from needing an electronic device to distract him from his current environment. As a couple, we decided that we could no longer be paralyzed by our circumstances or feelings.

Maybe this is you, and you have wallowed long enough in your emotional state. Choose freedom by seeking God's presence. The Bible says,

> Where the spirit of the Lord is, there is freedom.
>
> —2 Corinthians 3:17 (NIV)

Child of God, rise up and be who God called you to be. Do not hide from the world, the diagnosis, or the circumstance you are facing. God knew you could get through it by His strength.

> No, despite all these things, overwhelming victory is ours through Christ, who loved us.
>
> —Romans 8:37 (NLT)

You have been equipped to conquer your battle by proclaiming the victory within God's Word. I love how Romans 8:37 describes the victory as overwhelming through Christ. God's promises are still available to you, so go claim your victory.

DESPERATE

Desperate to find answers, truth, and understanding of the autistic diagnosis we were facing, we went to our first parent group meeting at Hudson's school. A whole group of exhausted parents sitting in a circle on these tiny hard chairs asking for help for their child. At this moment, I am so consumed and grieved for each parent that I am mostly crying. In the middle of a sentence starting and ending with the word, disabled; all of a sudden, something welled up inside of me like a holy indignation.

I looked over at Allen and most of the time all he has to do is look at me and he knows I am about to do something crazy. He is giving me the death stare like, *please do not embarrass me,* and my crazy self doesn't even care at that point. I said out loud to the group that day that I refused to feel hopeless in this situation and that this diagnosis would not limit my son. I said that I served a God capable of healing and restoration because the Bible says that by Jesus' stripes, my son can be healed. I also stated out loud that if they wanted to know about my God to talk to me after the meeting.

The public-school counselor leading the session probably thought, *okay—this chick is nuts, she cannot talk about God in public school, and cannot discriminate others by her faith or push her faith on someone else.* She quickly redirected the group and closed out the session with a novel of pamphlets on how to get help through a diagnosis of autism.

One of the parents came up to me after and said, with tears in her eyes, "Thank you for saying what you did." She proceeded to tell me that she was tired of feeling hopeless, too. We agreed to encourage and pray for one another.

Needless to say, my husband and I never got invited by the school to another parent meeting. Oh well, that was okay with me. Even among non-believers and negative circumstances, I was thankful for that spark of faith. After all, desperate times call for desperate measures, right?

Not long after our new diagnosis of autism, one of our close elderly family members passed away. I went to the funeral service and walked through the line to visit with family and friends after the service. As I was standing in line, my eyes caught sight of the lady who had prayed with my husband and me at the unforgettable couples' retreat a few years prior. The one who prayed over my womb. Do you remember my description of the fierce spiritual prayer warrior who felt like she could see through my soul when she prayed for me? Yes, it was her. I knew I had to talk to her. I not only wanted to thank her for praying with me before, but I really felt like I wanted her to pray with me about Hudson's diagnosis.

I walked right up to this lady, and she knew exactly who I was. She pulled me to the side, and we talked and prayed with each other. She encouraged me with declarations from God's Word over Hudson. She encouraged me to hang on to the promises of God and the miracles of the past. She knew the process for childbirth had been a difficult journey for us, and so she knew all the more of the despair we felt with a diagnosis of autism spoken over our miracle son.

How amazing is it that God would see and know my concern and pain enough to place someone I respected and looked up to as a prayer warrior, even during a funeral service for a mutual acquaintance? God seems to speak to me and through me in some of the strangest atmospheres it seems. Remember the gnat-filled tent revival and, of course, the parent-teacher conference earlier, and now a funeral?

> For I am sure that neither death nor life, nor angels nor rulers, nor things present nor things to come, nor powers, nor height nor depth, nor anything else in all creation, will be able to separate us from the love of God in Christ Jesus our Lord.
>
> —Romans 8:38-39 (ESV)

Your desperation for answers or comfort cannot compare to the desperation God has for our souls and a relationship with us. Sometimes passion results from desperation. Listen, friend, let us together use that passion to share the truth. There is always someone waiting for you to share the good news, the Gospel of Jesus in this dark world. Doom and gloom will always be in our worldly environment, but people are also hungry for hope. Know the Word of God so you can share it with someone desperate for peace. Some are in prison in their minds and they need to see someone else rise up and proclaim the victory. As children of God, we are now under a new covenant, and He adopted us into his family.

> For everyone who has been born of God overcomes the world. And this is the victory that has overcome the world, our faith. Who is it that overcomes the world except the one who believes that Jesus is the Son of God?
>
> —1 John 5:4-5 (ESV)

The generational curses that may have been passed down no longer have power because God's son died on the cross.

> "The thief comes only in order to steal and kill and destroy. I came that they may have and enjoy life, and have it in abundance [to the full, till it overflows]."
>
> —John 10:10 (ESV)

Maybe in my own despair, God tested my faith to see if I would choose to accept and live in defeat of my circumstances or continue to speak victory by faith even though the visible evidence did not support my faith. After all, the Bible defines faith by stating,

> Now faith is the substance of things hoped for, the evidence of things not seen.
>
> —Hebrews 11:1 (NKJV)

SHOCK

A few months passed by, and Charlotte was growing and developing her personality. I believe Charlotte was a gift from God. She has always had the ability to make me laugh when I have felt like crying. Charlotte has been my motivation to hold it together when I have felt like falling apart. Most importantly, she is living evidence of my divine healing as promised through the prophet during the infamous tent revival. Afterall, he did state that not only would I have a child but that I would have children.

Hudson was continuing to go to speech therapy with seemingly minimal improvements in his speech. Even though Hudson would have moments of crying, it mostly seemed to be out of frustration of not being able to communicate his needs. Hudson was a very loving child despite his diagnosis of autism. He is full of joy when we are not trying to force him to be like everyone else. He would give kisses to get his way because he knew that this was the way to all of his caregiver's hearts.

As for my new career change, six months after being in my new role as staff nurse, the current clinical coordinator left, and they asked me to take her place.

So, remember how I took a lateral move in my career and would likely never move up the clinical ladder? Think again!

When God has a plan, it is to prosper us, not to harm us or limit us. That role also came with a pay raise.

> Now unto him that is able to do exceedingly abundantly above all that we ask or think, according to the power that works in us.
>
> —Ephesians 3:20 (NKJV)

Do not be afraid to take that step of faith. Even during my chaos, God was still blessing me. It was shocking to me how quickly God blessed my career.

In January of 2017, we decided to put our home on the market in an effort to be closer to my parents' home. Honestly, we did not know what we would do, but we felt this urgency to sell our home. Soon after, we got an offer on our home, and it sold pretty fast. March of 2017, it was moving week and the closing of our home. We were in the middle of packing up our stuff with really no permanent home in mind yet.

We decided to move in with my parents in what we called "the love shack" (basically a garage with a loft, kitchenette, closet, and bathroom). We felt this would be a very temporary home since we had two small children in such a small space. As we were cleaning and moving out the last bit of our furniture, we got a phone call letting us know that my father-in-law was in a hospice setting, and he would be passing away soon. Allen's daddy had been suffering a sudden form of dementia that became debilitating. Allen loved his daddy very much, and even though we knew the dementia was sudden and incurable, we still were praying for a miracle.

Do you remember my women's Bible study group from earlier? They were, again, my tribe of support. They came to the rescue by packing up the rest of our home and cleaning it perfectly so that we could close as planned.

Allen's father passed away soon thereafter, and shock seemed to cause us to walk in a fog of chaos. Here we were with two small children, a diagnosis of autism, the loss of a parent, and moving into a very small space, all while trying to make sense of it all. Allen was bearing the weight of the world on his shoulders and the weight of being a strong father, husband, and provider while also processing grief in his own time.

We could not understand our current circumstances, but we had to rely on the promises of God's Word.

> Be strong and courageous. Do not be afraid or terrified
> because of them, for the Lord your God goes with you; he

will never leave you nor forsake you.

—Deuteronomy 31:6 (NIV)

I felt a lot of pressure, most likely self-induced, to take on all the home-life responsibilities so my husband could grieve. The truth was I had never experienced this kind of loss, and I did not know how to comfort him. However, I did know who could comfort him, the best, and that was the Holy Spirit.

...but the Comforter, which is the Holy Ghost, whom the Father will send in my name, he shall teach you all things, and bring all things to your remembrance, whatsoever I have said unto you.

—John 14:26 (KJV)

I can remember feeling so burdened for my husband that I made good use of the only closet in the love shack. I took a spot in the back of the closet and made it into my prayer closet. Did you know there is a scripture about a prayer room in the Bible?

But when you pray, go into your private room, shut your door, and pray to your Father, who is in secret. And your Father who sees in secret will reward you.

—Matthew 6:6 (CSB)

The prayer closet was a game-changer, not only for me but for my whole family. I knew we needed God to intervene on our behalf in so many areas. We could not let our emotions of shock and grief keep us captive as parents as a couple and as individuals.

One night, I was determined not to let the sun go down without a change of the atmosphere in the love shack. I told my husband he needed to go to the prayer closet, and I did not want him to come out until he had an encounter with God. He probably thought I was losing my mind at the time, but a little while passed by and God's presence came. You see, you may be reading this book and think that the presence of God is just something you have heard about in the stories of the Bible. You may not think that you have access to His presence, but you do. David said,

> you make known to me the path of life; you will fill me with joy in your presence, with eternal pleasures at your right hand.
>
> —Psalm 16:11 (NIV)

God's presence was manifested in the prayer room to my husband. He came out, we prayed together, and decided to push through our emotions and our circumstances so that we could be unified and filled with joy. In unity, we were in one mind and one accord. The prayer closet became our war room. We wrote scriptures all over the walls to help us process our emotions. We both wrote in a prayer journal to be specific in our prayers, but also to leave a legacy one day to both of our children and generations to come.

As we dedicated and honored God with time in the prayer closet, God began opening doors in our lives. One day, while I was searching online for a specific type of autism therapy that may help Hudson, ABA (Applied Behavioral Analysis), I stumbled across a private college not too far away that had an on-campus autism program with ABA therapy preschool. I called to try to get Hudson in that school right away, but we were placed on a waiting list because they only accept ten children into the program every year. God's favor came into play when it just so happened that Allen's sister had not long graduated from that college and had trained in that specific program. I continued to bug the director by email and phone, checking the status of our place on the waitlist. This private program would only accept certain insurances, and was very expensive to pay out of pocket. At the time, we had insurance that would not have been accepted.

Open enrollment for my husband's workplace was in May of 2017. This open enrollment period offered coverage with a different company than what we currently had. For the first time ever consistent in our state legislation, Adaptive Behavioral Treatment (ABT) services for this coverage plan were covered for members up to age nineteen who were diagnosed with an autism spectrum disorder, starting January 2017. We decided without knowing if we would get into the desired private autism preschool program of our choice that we should sign up with my husband's plan for the children's health insurance.

Months passed by, and we were still waiting to hear from the private school. My God is faithful! Sure enough, we did end up getting into this program in July of 2017. So, guess what? God knew that the program would be too expensive for us without the best insurance. God did not want us to live underneath mountains of debt, and He knew the desires of our hearts to get our son in what we believed was the best program in our state.

Friend, trust Him.

It was a miracle of not only being on a mile-long waiting list and getting accepted into the program, but also a miracle of getting a change of insurance during the perfect open enrollment period just two months prior to getting accepted into the program. God is always on time.

> Surely, Lord, you bless the righteous; you surround them with your favor as with a shield.
>
> —Psalm 5:12 (NIV)

Let me be clear, God did not do this for us because we were perfect, He did it because He loves His children.

Our emotions changed with the wind, but we hold on to the miracles of the past that God was the only constant. He was real, and He was faithful to His Word.

> For the Word of the Lord is upright, and all His work is done in faithfulness.
>
> —Psalm 33:4 (ESV)

We were overjoyed that God would hear our cries and allow us this opportunity to send our son to this program. Hudson never cried and seemed to love going to his new school. My mom drove him back and forth to school every day while she and my aunt made sure Charlotte was also taken care of so that I could still work. So many answered prayers all in the midst of painful circumstances.

I believe that it is in the painful seasons of our life that we mature in our faith. Think about farming and when farmers know they need to put fertilizer on their crops. Fertilizers are not fun, they literally stink, but it is only after the crops get fertilized that growth is visible.

We were hoping for a period of time to take a deep breath, maybe relax a little. Our season of pain and fertilization became a season of pruning as well.

Pruning is when a farmer cuts back the dead or overgrown branches in order to increase fruitfulness and growth. As the branch is being pruned, it may feel betrayed by the farmer. Maybe the branch cannot see how the pain of the cut can do any good. However, horticultural science proves the benefits of pruning by stimulating the growth and quality of fruit. Galatians 5:22 (KJV) describes the fruit of the Spirit,

> but the fruit of the Spirit is love, joy, peace, longsuffering, gentleness, goodness, faith, meekness, and temperance.

No one, including me, wants to think or talk about longsuffering.

In November of 2017, my mom called me at work and told me that my grandfather, "Pappy" as we called him, had a stroke. She told me that he was going to be taken to a hospital close by and if I wanted to see him to meet her there. My heart was breaking as I rushed out of the clinic. I got to the hospital, and I had my son Hudson with me. He had speech therapy that day, and I wanted him to still get to go, so I went into the hospital room and spoke to my Pappy. I gave him a hug and a kiss, and I told him I needed to take Hudson to therapy.

Pappy responded with his loving and caring-as-always demeanor, "Okay."

I told Hudson to say, "bye-bye Pappy," and he did! He said Pappy—which was new! My mom and grandmother were so happy to hear his words. We left to go to speech therapy encouraged about Hudson's words, but I was still concerned about Pappy's health. We knew all we could do was pray for healing and a miracle. My mom kept in touch with me and told me Pappy would be transferred to a university hospital about an hour away because his stroke was a bleeding stroke. My Pappy's condition was a rollercoaster. My mom, grandmother, and aunt all rotated and stayed night and day by his side.

My husband and I had to make childcare arrangements since my mom at the time was still the primary caregiver for our children as we worked. As time continued to pass, my Pappy, mom, and grandmother missed celebrating Hudson's fourth birthday that month. My mom came home from the hospital on the eve of Thanksgiving Day, and she got the call that Pappy had another stroke. She immediately had to go back to the hospital and our Thanksgiving Day was a solemn meal of shock. We also struggled to find consistent childcare which was not simple since my son was commuting ninety minutes round trip to his new ABA private school that we were so thrilled to get him into and our daughter was enrolled in a half-day preschool program at a church. Our family visited the hospital as often as we could; however, my mom and grandmother never left his side.

On December 23, 2017, my Pappy went to heaven. This was extraordinarily overwhelming as we were ending the year with having lost two family members—Allen's dad in March and my Pappy in December.

I had traveled the world with my Pappy and spent more nights with my grandparents than I probably did at my own house growing up. Allen, the children, and I would eat every Tuesday with my grandparents. We had such a close relationship, and I always wanted to model my marriage after theirs. My grandparents loved each other so much, and they always knew time spent with family was priceless.

To honor my Pappy, I wrote his obituary and made his programs for his funeral service. What was supposed to be a festive holiday season became a time of funeral gathering. To say shock and loss rocked our world that year is an understatement.

Our prayer closet and the day-to-day grace that we felt from God helped us survive 2017. I often felt in that season of my life, that my sensitivity and vulnerability made me feel weak or exposed, but it also allowed me to sympathize and relate to others on a much deeper level. I learned that people all around me were hurting and that as long as I was feeding my spirit with God's Word that I could in turn pour into other people with that light and hope.

> Praise be to the God and Father of our Lord Jesus Christ, the Father of compassion and the God of all comfort, who comforts us in all our troubles, so that we can comfort those in any trouble with the comfort we ourselves receive from God. For just as we share abundantly in the sufferings of Christ, so also our comfort abounds through Christ. If we are distressed, it is for your comfort and salvation; if we are comforted, it is for your comfort, which produces in you patient endurance of the same sufferings we suffer. And our hope for you is firm, because we know that just as you share in our sufferings, so also you share in our comfort.
>
> —2 Corinthians 1:3-7 (NIV)

Our Savior, Jesus Christ suffered more than any of us can even imagine. He is the only true one that can empathize and comfort us in loss, pain, and hurt. I can not stress enough that a relationship with God and His Word is the key in growing in spiritual maturity. No one wants to go through suffering of any kind, and unfortunately, we live in a world that is full of suffering and darkness. Oppression has rooted deep roots of bitterness throughout generations and caused great division. We are witnessing this now in a climate of high racial tension but this is not new. Look back in the Bible all the way back to the Old Testament, the Israelites were a people accustomed to slavery and oppression. We must learn as children of God to break the chains of bondage and suffering by clinging to the light. Jesus Christ is the only one who can save us. If we can continue to fill ourselves up with God's Word, we can shine His light.

The dark world we are living in does not want our opinions or condemnation. They are starved for light and love. Jesus loved first; He spoke the truth in love and He is the only one who can heal the sin and change the hearts of all mankind.

> For it is the God who commanded light to shine out of darkness, who has shone in our hearts to give the light of the knowledge of the glory of God in the face of Jesus Christ.
>
> —2 Corinthians 4:6 (NKJV)

WEARY

In 2018, we were still trying to figure out our timeline and plans regarding buying or building a new home. We were so cramped in the love shack, and frankly it became pretty uncomfortable. We ate most of our meals with my parents due to our tight living space and felt like we had nowhere to truly relax. Charlotte, our now two-year-old, slept in the middle of our bed every night; our one closet was soon taken over by children's clothes, tubs of our own clothes, and shoes galore. It was easier at this point to buy new clothes than it was to look for something that may or may not have been washed or pulled out of storage. The love shack needed ventilation and the air was so damp that our children began getting croupy coughs and colds constantly. We cringed at the thought of a visitor and we felt as though privacy was non-existent during this season. The season of waiting for a home was never meant to last this long.

Our desire to find a more permanent home seemed to grow more with every passing day. Every time we went to look at homes nothing seemed to work out. No home that we looked at met our needs. The budget was not right, the school district was not right, or the neighborhood was not where we felt God wanted us. So much frustration we felt and hated to feel like we may be a burden to my parents who were supposed to be empty nesters. We were trying really hard to make the best of our situation and living area but it was hard, and it put a strain on us as individuals and as a couple.

I can remember wandering in this obstacle course of clothes, furniture, and toys galore to get to the prayer closet. Allen and I consistently felt the need to go to the closet. As tight as this space was, when we could get to His feet in worship and prayer, the troubles of the world would seem to lift. I cannot express enough how refreshing God's presence was when we would spend that time with Him.

Because of the Lord's great love we are not consumed, for

his compassions never fail. They are new every morning; great is your faithfulness. I say to myself, "The Lord is my portion; therefore, I will wait for him."

—Lamentations 3:22-24 (NIV)

All in the while of our current circumstantial living arrangements and the grief that we were both still dealing with, God was still blessing us. Our son, Hudson was doing well at school and seemed to be making progress. Charlotte was enjoying spending so much time with her grandparents and great-grandmother. Allen and I were so busy at work, and God blessed both of us in our careers in 2018. My manager at the time moved to another practice, and I was honored to be her replacement for the practice manager role in the office. My husband received several awards in his job that year. I had to learn a lot in my new role at work, and I was so thankful for the opportunity God had given me.

You see, in 2015, when God challenged my faith by calling me away from where I was comfortable in my career into a new career, He had a plan all the while. This plan allowed me to advance my career fast. I quickly had gone from staff nurse, to clinical coordinator, to practice manager. I truly believe that God opened each door for me and always had my best interest in mind. Work was never easy but I learned a tremendous amount and grew professionally. I developed lifetime friendships and relationships within the corporation. In my office at work I had the verse written,

Whatever you do, work at it with your whole being, for the Lord and not for men.

—Colossians 3:23 (BSB)

In 2018, my husband and I decided that it was time for us to make a decision regarding where we would live permanently. After much prayer we felt it would be best to build. My family had land that they

gifted to us close behind their home. We met with a builder and got all of our plans in order.

I believe that every person you meet in your lifetime is for a specific reason and purpose. Back in 2017 when we sold our home, the realtor that we used was married to a general contractor. He became our first choice as a contractor because he and his wife were so good to us when we sold our first home. The first time we met together for this project, he knew I was a dreamer and could tell almost instantly that he would have to reign me in with my desired designs. I told him that we prayed for this day, and that he would be amazed because God was our provider. I believed God would perform supernatural miracles, even down to the supplies needed to build our home. He probably thought I was nuts, but I did not care. The builder offered to build our home with little to no profit for himself.

My husband and I knew that this home that we were building would be a sanctuary for our family. We wanted to make Jesus the center of it all. When the house was framed, my husband and I wrote scripture all over the wood. We also placed a Bible in the foundation of the home. God's Word was so important to us because we knew that it was only by His mercy and grace that we had made it this far. We must cling to the promises and victories of the past to get us through the present and future. Even though the building process was just getting started, it was still encouraging to see some progress in one aspect of our lives.

It is very easy to grow weary in waiting. Maybe you are waiting for your miracle right now. Maybe you are waiting for your future spouse, a child, a home, a job, an answer, a family, a calling. Whatever you are waiting for there is a lot of scripture in the Bible that can encourage you while you wait.

> They who wait for the Lord shall renew their strength; they shall mount up with wings like eagles; they shall run and not be weary; they shall walk and not faint
>
> —Isaiah 40:31 (ESV)

> ...and let us not be weary in well doing; for in due season
> we shall reap, if we faint not.
>
> —Galatians 6:9 (KJV)

The year 2018 was a long year of waiting for us. Progress for our son seemed positive but slower than we hoped. Our speech therapist seemed to have lost his luster for helping Hudson. Therapy results became stagnant and it was to the point that Hudson's school teacher felt it was best for us to change speech therapist agencies. We did some research and all agreed on the change. With promising conversations our decision was made and we were thankful for this change.

Still though, we waited. We waited for the restoration of words. Every time I would get to my breaking point emotionally and spiritually it was as if God knew He would have to give me a glimpse of hope.

One day I was praying in the closet for Hudson, and I was so angry and weary that I didn't even know how to pray so I sat there. I got a message on my phone at 6:30 in the morning while I was sulking, and it was from a friend and family member that said she had the most amazing dream about Hudson that night. She said she dreamed he was saying lots of words and phrases. She said she was so encouraged she had to tell me even though it was so early in the morning.

Not only did this encourage me and renew my strength and hope, it also taught me the importance of obedience to the leading of the Spirit of God in all things. How awkward can you imagine that she may have felt texting me that early in the morning about a dream? When God asks you to do something, often it is unconventional, against our normal tendencies, and well-worth the risk. She was led by the Spirit to encourage me, and it gave me the strength to keep living and keep waiting.

No assignment from God is too minimal, it could be the moment God uses you to help someone from taking their own life. God is searching for a people who are eager to share the Gospel for the kingdom. Do not grow weary, and do not get cold feet in your assignment; do not let the devil talk you out of the task because of your comfort level. God chose you for that very moment.

But Samuel replied: "Does the LORD delight in burnt offerings and sacrifices as much as in obeying the LORD? To obey is better than sacrifice, and to heed is better than the fat of rams."

—1 Samuel 15:22 (NIV)

So many times, in my own life have I felt that I was not strong enough, wise enough, worthy enough to be used by God. However, oftentimes I have been reminded that *God does not usually call the qualified, he qualifies the called.*

Today, be encouraged as a woman of God, that you are never too far from His Holy Spirit who calls you. Scripture in Acts 2:39 (NIV) says,

for the promise is to you and to your children, and to all who are afar off, as many as the Lord our God will call.

Do not lose hope while waiting for clarity because you are just one step in faith away from your destiny in Christ. Even though we doubt His promises at times in our own lives because we grow weary while waiting, He is always faithful.

Take a good look at my servant. I'm backing him to the hilt. He's the one I chose, and I couldn't be more pleased with him. I've bathed him with my Spirit, my life. He'll set everything right among the nations.

—Isaiah 42:1 (MSG)

Isaiah is speaking of Jesus, our Redeemer, he says God chose Him and in the same way, He has chosen us and when we invite Jesus in our hearts, we have full privilege to His Holy Spirit and the same promises are for us.

WORRIED

The year 2018 proved to be a year of waiting for our family, but thankfully at this point, we had broken ground and were about half-way through the process of building our new home. We started off 2019 believing for the best year yet; after all, we would move into our new home this year. I had a blast getting to plan and design and build our home. My mom and I were constantly looking in magazines and watching all the home improvement shows on television. We spent a lot of time together trying to pick out every detail.

While spending a lot of time together, it shed light on some areas of concern I had for my mom. She was still grieving the loss of her father, my pappy, and she was not coping well. She was stuck in a pit of sadness that scared me. Every time I would talk to her about my concerns, we would argue and fight. I was so worried about her because I could see the toll the grief was playing on her, not only mentally and spiritually but also physically. She slowly isolated herself from church friends and church services. It was very strange to me because all my life she had been very insistent on staying involved in church. She taught Sunday school in her younger days and sang in the choir for as long as I could remember. She was a greeter at our church and always went to the annual couples' retreat. Now, mom would say she just did not feel like going to church, or she could only stay for a little while and she would leave.

One day, I asked her why she shut down every time we would bring up God or church, and she finally admitted that she was mad at God for allowing Pappy to die. For a year she tried to bury her anger and grief to appear strong for my family and my children. I could not help but think that with our family practically living with her and my dad for the last two years that we were hindering her healing.

Months passed and things seemed to get worse. It was to the point that I was not at peace with her keeping my children anymore. I was worried about their safety because she was battling with depression and coping in an unhealthy way. I had never seen my mom like this.

This was supposed to be a happy time for my family, knowing that we were very close to completing and moving into our forever home, and I could not even relax because I was so worried about my mom and children. Mom became angry with me because her perspective was that I was constantly preaching to her. I thought if I quoted enough scripture to her, that she would get over this grief and see the wealth of blessings before her.

Everything got worse.

She did not need me to quote scripture to her; she needed unconditional love and care from me. I knew that in order for her to heal, I would have to find another alternative for childcare, even if it was temporary. There was no way she could heal without being able to take time to take care of herself.

One warm spring day while volunteering at our church's annual golf tournament, our new pastor's wife was there, and I got the chance to sit down with her and get to know her. During our conversation which I thought would likely just be an ice-breaker, she spoke words of wisdom that to this day I cannot forget. She shared her testimony about her life with me, and what she spoke most of was a difficult relationship with her mother. She told me if she had to go through that experience again, she would have just shown love more, even when it was not fair or justified. The power of forgiveness and love could heal relationships and souls. It resonated with me instantly, and I knew in that moment God was speaking to me. I never told her about my mom and my concerns, so this was even more of a reason to believe that God was teaching me something that day.

My mom's situation still was not improving, and it became harder and harder to talk to her. Every time I could feel anger and resentment welling up inside of me, that conversation with our pastor's wife would remind me to just show love and forgiveness.

Be kind to one another, tenderhearted, forgiving one

LINDSAY STONE CORBETT

another, as God in Christ forgave you.

—Ephesians 4:32 (ESV)

Forgiving someone does not necessarily mean that they were not wrong towards you; it means you are releasing the pain of the hurt and not holding it against the person. If you choose not to, a root of bitterness, resentment, and eventually guilt will grow deep into the soil of your heart.

In all honesty, how can any of us hold back on forgiveness when Jesus Christ has forgiven us and pardoned us by giving his life on a cross. He paid the price of all our sins, and he forgives us daily.

...for you, O Lord, are good and forgiving, abounding in steadfast love to all who call upon you.

—Psalm 86:5 (ESV)

Is there someone that you are withholding forgiveness to that has never apologized to you? That is the person you need to forgive. Let go of the pain of the hurt by pardoning your offender's actions, and let God restore your joy and kindness so that you may have no regrets. I never said it would be easy and neither did God. In fact, for me it became harder every passing day to show grace. So many times I had to bite my tongue, walk away, and try to distance myself in order not to sin in my responses.

On Good Friday 2019, I was in tears, worried sick about my mom. I can remember being in the love shack, just crying out to God asking him to heal my mom. I wanted God to open her eyes so that she could see what the pain of her grief was doing to her and her family. I begged God for continued protection, direction, and peace.

I was exhausted mentally and just decided to sit and wait. I was looking at social media and scrolling at pictures, and in that moment I felt God speak to my Spirit, "Why have you not thought about her?" He was referring to a young woman who was newer in our lives and was married but did not have children. I knew very little about her, but I knew God was telling me to reach out to her. There have only been a handful of times in my life when I knew God was answering a prayer instantly, and this was one of those times. I was not even friends with her on social media, but I found her and sent her a message asking if she was available to help us with our children in any way, shape, or form. I gave her the logistics and complexity of our schedules and commutes to Hudson's school and Charlotte's preschool. She responded quickly and told me that she was actually searching for a full-time nanny position. She said that she was preparing for an interview that was later that exact day. She said that she did not have peace about that position or family, and was praying for God to help her find the right family. She was so eager and amazed at how God spoke to me and to her, in this very moment. Allen and I were in a unified agreement that we had to do this for our family.

I was so afraid that my mom would resent me forever and think I was calling her incompetent or that I was ungrateful for all the years of dedication she had given to my family. I dreaded the conversation with my mom, but I was so thankful and amazed at how fast God worked in that situation. I knew the nanny was the answer to my prayers, and I knew this would give mom the time she needed to heal her wounded spirit. She surprisingly took the news of the nanny better than I thought, but it was still uncomfortable. There were several awkward moments of silence, especially since we were still living with my parents. My dad was supportive of the nanny because he knew mom was struggling with depression.

On Easter Sunday, mom spoke to all of us at Sunday lunch that something the pastor said during the service spoke to her and showed her that she needed help in order to heal. This was the first Sunday she had sat in church for the entire service in a year or more. I will never forget that she was sitting on the back row. I was amazed that the Holy Spirit loved her so much that he found her, penetrated her thirsty soul, and she finally surrendered to His will.

I am reminded of the story of the woman at the well; it took an undeniable encounter with Jesus for her to know the love that God had for her. It took that moment to show her the goodness of God. My mom was no different. She had been hurt by life's circumstances and was stuck in her emotional bondage until Jesus came for her.

> "Suppose one of you has a hundred sheep and loses one of them. Doesn't he leave the ninety-nine in the open country and go after the lost sheep until he finds it? And when he finds it, he joyfully puts it on his shoulders and goes home. Then he calls his friends and neighbors together and says, 'Rejoice with me; I have found my lost sheep."
>
> —Luke 15:4-6 (NIV)

We were all so thankful that God rescued her mind, and she was finally open to the idea that she needed help to heal. I will not lie and pretend that I was a little skeptical of her statement, because I would need to see a change in her behavior in order to know if she was changed. My mom's eyes were opened instantly, but she was not delivered instantly. I was still ecstatic that she was at least trying.

As time passed, mom had ups and downs, highs and lows, but steadily she was improving. She received counseling and began to seek after God again. She started back going to church consistently and working through her grief. We had some very good conversations during that time. Our relationship was now healing. Mom was able to spend priceless time with my grandmother, and they enjoyed gardening, shopping, and traveling. Mom had no restrictions on her time or schedule because we hired the nanny. The nanny was an answer to so many prayers.

> Every good and perfect gift is from above, coming down from the Father of the heavenly lights, who does not change like shifting shadows.
>
> —James 1:17 (NIV)

God is constant, unwavering, and unchanging in His love and pursuit for us.

ENCOURAGED

The nanny we hired in 2019 was able to take excellent care of our children. God not only answered our prayers about my mom and childcare provision, but he saved my mother's soul. You see, He longs to spend eternity with us so much that He is willing to rescue us and save us, even in our lowest moments. He loves us so much that He sent Jesus to pay the price of our sin on the cross. I am forever grateful to God for saving my mom from the torment and bondage that she was in.

Months passed by and my mom was herself again. It was like a complete turn-around for the better. The tides had changed in our family and we were all mending and healing together. As a family things were looking up for us and we were happy and looking forward to our next family summer vacation.

Right before our annual family vacation, chaos hit, and fear challenged our faith once more; out of nowhere, our son Hudson started feeling sick with nausea and vomiting. We were trying our best to deal with the sickness at home and with conservative measures since we thought it was just a stomach virus. Hudson's symptoms did not show signs of improvement, so my mom and I took Hudson to the pediatrician's office. They drew lab work on Hudson and his blood work indicated a high white blood cell count (which showed an infection) and his blood sugar was a little low at the doctor's office.

I can still to this day feel the panic that I felt in that moment. I looked at my mom and my eyes welled up. Despite all the circumstances my mom always knew how to reassure and comfort me that Hudson would be okay. The doctor thought that the symptoms would improve and hopefully he would be back to normal soon.

Hudson has always been a very picky eater. He is also sensitive to different textures of foods which can make variety difficult. He only drank almond milk and water, which made hydration and vitamin replenishment difficult during this sickness. He continued to vomit and soon resisted all food. It was very scary to us as parents, but we thought *surely, he is on the mend.* We prayed night and day for him, but it still was not improving.

That Sunday morning, my husband and Charlotte went to church, but Hudson and I stayed home so I could monitor his symptoms. He was still very sick. Hudson suddenly grew very pale, and his breathing was shallow. He was difficult to arouse and keep awake. I frantically notified my husband and told him we must take Hudson to the emergency room, and quickly.

We went to the nearest children's emergency room; it was the same one we went to four years earlier around the same time of the year when Hudson got sick then. So many horrible reminders of his previous emergency room experience flooded my mind. I was determined not to let it become a similar experience.

I was a wreck emotionally, and we called our pastor and church and family to pray for Hudson to be healed. We recited scriptures from the Bible:

...by His stripes we are healed.

— Isaiah 53:5 (NKJV)

No weapon that is forged against you will be effective. This is the heritage of the LORD's servants, and their righteousness from me," says the LORD.

—Isaiah 54:17 (ISV)

When they checked Hudson's blood sugar it was only fifty-four; that is very low for a child, and he was very sick. We had no idea why his blood sugar was that low other than just he was not able to eat without getting sick. The doctors and staff ran several tests all which revealed nothing other than dehydration and low blood sugar. They gave him some medications and intravenous solutions to help him overcome the nausea, and we were trying everything they had to offer to get him to eat.

We were supposed to go on our family vacation the next day, but we were so torn on what to do. The doctors did not want to admit Hudson; they thought due to his improving current condition, he would likely continue to improve at home. They discharged us home with no more knowledge of what was going on, but we knew we had to keep a close eye on him at all times.

I can remember stopping at a fast food restaurant and telling my husband to get anything we thought Hudson would eat. I bought chocolate, and liquid sweeteners to try to sustain his blood sugar. *Why is God allowing my son to suffer like this?* It was hard enough that Hudson normally had limited communication with us; this only made our anxiety about how he was feeling when he was sick greater. We pled the blood of Jesus over Hudson's body, calling all of his organs and cells in line with God's Word, declaring that he would be healed of this sickness. We decided the next day that we would head to the beach since it was only a couple hours away, and because Hudson seemed to improve some overnight.

Every year my family—including my parents, grandmother, and siblings—have always gone to the beach for a week together. We especially hated to miss our family vacation, even with Hudson's sickness. I knew I would have more support being with my family than stuck at home worrying myself to death about Hudson's progression of healing. In years past our beach trips were filled with stories of places we stayed in that were crammed so tight and may have even seemed like a cave but it did not matter. As long as we were all together and at the beach, all was well. My parents loved being at the beach, and they loved the quality time that we would all spend together.

This year, for whatever reason, my mom pulled out all the stops for the annual family beach trip. She rented the nicest beach house we had ever had the opportunity to stay in. It was magnificent, and we were all at a good place emotionally and relationally with each other as a family. My sister and her husband had a nine month old baby and they were there. My brother and his wife, who had suffered a miscarriage the previous year, were pregnant again, and during that week they revealed the gender of their baby. My parents were over the moon excited to gain another grandson. They revealed their baby name and would name him after my sister in law's grandfather and our pappy. My mom was thrilled that they would use Pappy's name.

By this time, Hudson's health was improving but still not at one hundred percent. However, we were still so thankful to God that he allowed Hudson's health to improve throughout that week. This vacation ended up being the best family beach week we had ever experienced. Everyone had a great time together, the food was delicious, the beach was awesome, and even the weather was perfect. To top it all off, by the time we left the beach, Hudson seemed to be getting back to his normal self.

When we got home from vacation, all of us went back to work, and thankfully our nanny was still caring for our children while we worked. My mom was doing great physically, spiritually, and emotionally now. We even felt comfortable enough to let mom take Charlotte to play and swim in a neighbor's pool. She laughed and told us about all the fun they had playing with some of Charlotte's cousins. My mom and grandmother continued their gardening adventures and even planned a few sporadic day trips to the beach. It was starting to feel like a great summer.

Our new home was very close to completion, furniture had been purchased, and we were only days away from getting to move in. Everyone was so excited. When we were still in the process of building our home I felt God speak to me, "I am preparing a table for you."

> "You prepare a table before me in the presence of my enemies; You anoint my head with oil; My cup runs over."
>
> —Psalm 23:5 (NKJV)

I was thankful that I sensed God speaking to me, but the revelation of what that verse would mean was not yet revealed to me. Oftentimes, God speaks in the still small voice and this was one of those moments.

The Lord said, "Go out and stand on the mountain in the presence of the Lord, for the Lord is about to pass by. Then a great and powerful wind tore the mountains apart and shattered the rocks before the Lord, but the Lord was not in the wind. After the wind there was an earthquake, but the Lord was not in the earthquake. After the earthquake came a fire, but the Lord was not in the fire. And after the fire came a gentle whisper.

—1 Kings 19:11-12 (NIV)

If you question hearing or knowing when God is speaking to you, read your Bible. God's Word is right there in front of you. Keep seeking and He will reveal to you knowledge that you, in your own natural mind, could not have understood. Biblical scholars and fellow believers have described this concept as revelation knowledge. It can seem as if the scriptures leap off the page and alert your supernatural spiritual awareness. God's Word will reveal that knowledge to you if you meditate on the scriptures enough for them to light-up in your heart and spirit.

Light up, shine, and show up like glitter on the page. Even during happy times it is important for us to stay focused and plugged into our source of power, God.

In early August, I felt the need to go on a social media fast. I knew that in order to keep my spirit in tune with God's, I would have to turn off the distractions of this world. I had not realized how much time I was wasting on social media. Oftentimes, it was the last thing I looked at before going to bed and the first thing I might check in the morning. Those notifications would spark my curiosity instantly, and then twenty minutes later I scrolled through other folks' drama and listened to everything the world had to say. I could have been spending that time reading God's Word or praying, and then I would know more of what God was saying.

If you feel like your filter is clogged and you doubt hearing His voice, then I advise you to evaluate what you are feeding your body, soul, and spirit. What goes in and comes out—good, bad, or ugly. Twenty-one days of freedom from social media would do my soul good and allow me to acknowledge the presence of God in my life. Overall, I was encouraged that, as a family, we had a happy time together and that good things were in store for us.

BEWILDERED

One hot August Sunday, I begged my mom to go with me back to the local home improvement store to pick out a stain for our deck that was being completed that week. She told me she was not feeling well, and she said she felt really nauseous and weak. I asked her to make an appointment with her doctor that week because I was concerned about her. She said she would, and then she mustered up enough strength to head to the store as I had requested along with me, Charlotte, and my grandmother. We wandered through the store, and I noticed mom was having a difficult time trying to smile through her discomfort as we looked at endless paint and stain colors. We found what we were looking for and headed back home.

The next day, everyone went back to their daily routines, and mom still was not feeling well but just thought maybe she had a virus or something. She made an appointment with her doctor for later that day.

On Tuesday of that very week, as I was pulling out the driveway, I heard God speak to my soul. He said, "Sometimes I take people early because they have completed their assignment on earth." I thought to myself, *that was a good word. He must want me to share that with our nanny since she had lost her father less than a year prior to meeting our family.* I planned to text that to her later to remind her of the goodness of God, but like most, I got busy and distracted and forgot to send the message.

While I was at work, I started to doubt my deck stain color that we picked out on Sunday, and I knew the builder would be coming soon to stain the deck. I remember calling my mom that day around ten in the morning to ask if she could pick up the stain, take it back to the store, and ask for a darker color. As she spoke, I knew she sounded like she was not feeling well.

When I questioned the sound of her voice, she said, "I will be fine." She said she would try to go by the store when she got the time.

My husband went by our new house and was casually checking

in with what work was being completed that day because we were so excited to move in very soon. While he was at the house, his car broke down. Of course, he called my mom—she was always eager to help—and asked her if she could come and pick him up and take him to get someone to look at the car. She did not hesitate to say yes, but she was with my grandmother at this point. She told my grandmother she really was not feeling well and asked if my grandmother would go get Allen. So, my grandmother left and went to get my husband from the new house. My grandmother told Allen that my mom was pretty sick and that she was going to go with her to the doctor.

They went to the doctor's office, and the doctor was not as alarmed as my grandmother and my mom were about her symptoms. By this time, my mom was having abdominal and arm pain and could not hold any food or drink down and was extremely weak. My mom and grandmother asked the doctor if they felt she needed to go to the hospital. They said no, that they would give her some nausea medication and that she could go home and try to eat and drink. If she did not improve, then she should go to the emergency room.

They left the doctor's office and headed to my grandmother's house. My grandmother let my mom rest and tried to encourage her to eat or drink. Mom felt so bad that she did not think she could even go to the pharmacy and pick up her medicine. My mom called my father to ask if he would pick up her prescriptions from the pharmacy on his way home from work. She decided to stay at my grandmother's house and attempt to rest while she waited for my dad to pick her up because she did not have the strength to drive.

I did not know all that was going on or how sick my mother actually was. I was home from work, and I made supper for us. Allen came home from work and ate supper. My dad called Allen to ask if he would ride over to my grandmother's house with him to get mom so they would not have to leave an extra car at my grandmother's house. He agreed, and they left.

All during this time, I had placed my phone under the bed on the charger, and it was off. A significant amount of time passed after I gave the kids their baths. I remember thinking that they should all be home by now. I never got really concerned because it was not out of character for my family to lose track of time while talking. I was standing at the sink in the love shack washing all the dishes from supper when all of a sudden, there was a banging on the door.

Startled, I opened it up, and it was my cousin. He was crying and saying, "Hurry up Lindsay, your mom is not breathing!" I was completely shocked and very emotional, crying, trying to gather my stuff and get the kids and put them in the car. I found my phone and there were a ton of missed calls and text messages from Allen. My dad and my husband had found my mom in my grandmother's bed, unresponsive.

I was sobbing all the way to my grandmother's and Charlotte my three-year-old said, "It is okay Mommy, Nana was a child of God. She is in heaven with Pappy and Papa John." I wailed all the more.

> Out of the mouth of babes and nursing infants You have ordained strength, Because of Your enemies, That You may silence the enemy and the avenger.
>
> —Psalm 8:2 (NKJV)

The faith that a child has is inspiring. The genuine and innocent faith and trust that children have in God is the way we all should approach His throne. Charlotte had no fear, worry, or despair as I did, even in the midst of terror and heartbreak, because she knew that her Nana was not lost but found. Charlotte knew that my mom was with her creator and all those who had passed before her in heaven.

We pulled up in the driveway of my grandmother's house; there were ambulances, police cars, and lights flashing. My cousin said, "I have the kids; go in the house and see your mom."

I ran, screamed, cried, and bulldozed in the house wailing, "My mom, my mom!"

Allen and my dad had tried to do CPR (cardiopulmonary resuscitation) on her but were never able to feel a pulse or see a breath. They called 911, and the medical staff came and tried to do the same prior to my arrival. My grandmother was horrified. This was a complete nightmare. They said she is gone; she is dead. I could not believe this! I had talked to her that day. I threw myself over her body and prayed and begged God to raise her from the dead.

My grandmother told us that she had just told her she was going to go take a hot bath, and then she was going to lay down to try to go to sleep so she could hopefully feel better. Apparently, she laid down and never woke up.

The police and medical staff examined her and felt that it was a sudden cardiac death or heart attack. They found nothing suspicious about it all and were ready to take her to the morgue. My siblings came to my grandmother's and so many family members and friends. By this time, it was around eight-thirty or nine in the evening.

For the longest time, we cried and laid there, hoping that God would heal her just as he did with Lazarus. She did not come back to us. It is sickening even to this day to relive this moment.

Here I was, this nurse and daughter who could not even take care or help my own mother. I am certified in CPR; if only I could have gotten there earlier, maybe I could have brought her back. I always had my phone close by; the one time I do not, this is what happens! Why did her doctor not realize she was obviously having signs or symptoms of a heart attack? So many terrifying thoughts and what-ifs still ring in my mind even to this day.

To say that we were all in shock would be a huge understatement. My mom was the glue that held our family together. She was everything to us; she took care of all of us all the time. She was extravagant, beautiful, and vibrant on every level. Everyone who knew her recognized her beauty and flair. We were all devastated by the loss of my mom. Our summer that had all seemed so great was spiraling down to this huge moment of sorrow.

DEVASTATED

As soon as she passed, it was like my world was spinning out of control. I think we all stayed at my grandmother's house until four o'clock in the morning. We eventually left and went to my parents' home to try to sleep and just sat there in a daze of grief. We were getting calls constantly from the morgue, the funeral home, organ donor associations.

Me, my sister, aunt, and grandmother went that morning to the finest dress shop within a forty-five-mile radius and bought her the most beautiful and expensive outfit. My mom was a fashionista, and we wanted her to look just as fabulous as she always did as people peered into her casket.

Multiple visitors, casseroles, desserts, hugs, and tears passed as quickly as the time did. I had to write an obituary, plan a funeral, order flowers, take care of everything because I knew how mom would want it all. I wanted to please her so bad, for some reason, and tried to think like her in all of the planning.

What a nightmare it all was as I think back, but all of my family could agree on one thing: we were so thankful that God intervened in mom's life and saved her soul from self-destruction just a few months earlier. We were so thankful that we had the best family vacation that year, and that there were no unresolved hard feelings between us.

I found my mom's Bible, and in it she had written songs that she wanted to be played or sang at her own funeral. She had scriptures written that helped her in her darkest times. All similar scriptures that you have read so far in this book. I never knew that she would leave us so soon. Her funeral was packed with people, a seemingly endless procession flooded the altar of our church. Each time someone came by me, I would burst into tears, and they would embrace me and try to offer kind sentiments. Nothing seemed to take the pain away, though.

I would have to cling to one promise: God loved her enough to save her soul so that she could spend eternity with Him and so that we could see her again someday in heaven.

I was trying to make every detail of her funeral arrangements just as she would want it. We picked out the most gorgeous flowers, a slideshow with as many pictures as we could find, a full choir, and some of the best preachers, including my brother. My brother was a policeman until he became a youth pastor at our home church not long before mom passed away. He had the honor of speaking at mom's funeral. My husband, family, and friends rallied around me, helping me stand when I was weak. I could stay in this chapter with every detail of every emotion that I felt during this time, but I will spare you from the agony. The bottom line is that I had to rely on God for strength and motivation in the season I was in.

I reflect back on the awesome way God allowed my mom and grandmother to spend all that time together, how we were able to live with my parents even in the seemingly bad days, and how He worked in aligning my path to meet our nanny and already have that established. *How could we have functioned without that already in place?* He allowed my mom to be with us in all the planning and construction of our new home. Believe me, my family and I have analyzed this event endlessly and despite our regrets, sadness, and anger, we still know God was in control.

A week of funeral plans passed by, and the grief was really only beginning. I was having a very difficult time trying to be strong in front of my children and trying not to stay lost in my sadness. I became very depressed and angry on the inside while trying to keep it together.

My life seemed to be living in fast forward. Right after the funeral services, it was time for us to move into our home. This was extremely painful to do without my mom. I was relying on her to help me arrange all the furniture and hang all the pictures, and if there was any woman that knew how to work to get the job done, it was her. We had plans of painting antique furniture and table arrangements, decorating, and all the details. I was trying so hard to push forward for the sake of my children and family, but I was slowly falling to pieces all over again. I was broken.

What was supposed to be this awesome plan of moving into our forever home ended up being continuous moments of missing mom.

I often wondered if Hudson understood what was going on or if he would remember her. I knew Charlotte seemed so strong the night of her passing in her reassuring child-like faith as she spoke comfort to my weary soul. However, I did wonder if she really understood that Nana would not be back with us here on earth. Charlotte asked endless questions along the way. So many nights, I would lie awake crying in Charlotte's bed after she would fall to sleep. I would wipe away my tears and then head off to my bedroom. Allen would embrace me and try to encourage me with one of his famous pep-talks to keep me going.

CONSUMED

After the funeral, I took a couple of weeks off from work but then soon returned to work. While at work, there were so many days that I felt like I was barely surviving mentally. I had an awesome work family that offered comfort and support throughout the day. I was also so very thankful for the nanny who was holding my hand through all of this. She could understand my feelings due to her recent loss of a parent. She seemed to know just what to say. She was not just a nanny for my children so I could work, but also a friend to me.

A few days passed, and just as I was getting settled back into work, the nanny called me and said that Charlotte was screaming and crying and saying her head hurt so bad. The nanny said she had never seen her like this and she was scared. I told her I would meet her at the emergency room—the same emergency room that Hudson had been at in July. I called Allen and told him the news. I was in tears, crying all the way to the hospital.

When my husband and I got to the emergency room, Charlotte was still crying and screaming. All I could think of was the worst. *Oh God, please do not let her have a brain tumor or cancer. I cannot lose my baby girl. I just lost my mom. Why do we have to ride this crazy emotional rollercoaster of life?*

The medical staff were so good to us, and they gave Charlotte a thorough work-up—she was very brave. My three year old showed more faith and strength than I did. We prayed scriptures of healing over her and claimed that we would believe the report of the Lord.

> Heal me, O Lord, and I will be healed; save me and I will be saved, for you are the one I praise.
>
> —Jeremiah 17:14 (NIV)

"But I will restore you to health and heal your wounds,"
declares the LORD.

—Jeremiah 30:17 (NIV)

"He himself bore our sins" in his body on the cross, so that
we might die to sins and live for righteousness; "by his
wounds you have been healed."

—1 Peter 2:24 (NIV)

After multiple tests and a negative CT scan, we were relieved and thankful for a good report. They never could find a cause for the headache and chalked it up to a "psycho-somatic" event, likely related to all the emotional trauma and chaos she had gone through in recent weeks. I could not help but wonder, "why, God?"

I think a lot of people ask God questions; oftentimes these questions do not get answered, but they do help us process our circumstances. The Bible is full of people with questions for God. Just look at David in the book of Psalms. He asked a lot of "why me, God" questions when he was hurting, broken, and shamed. God cares about us, and He already knows our thoughts, so He allows us graciously to ask these questions. Sometimes God answers us, and sometimes He does not. It does not mean that He is not present with us. In His sovereignty, He still loves us and is working behind the scenes on our behalf— molding us and shaping us into who He has called us to be.

When the nanny called me at work, the first person I wanted to call was my mom. She had also been a nurse, and she would have met us at the emergency room and told all those doctors what they needed to be doing because that is just who she was. She was bold and always determined to make sure her family received the best care possible.

One Sunday church service, not long after mom passed away, I snuck in service to try to avoid having to talk to anyone. I remember going in on the side entrance and sitting there with Allen. At the end of the service, my family all ended up at the altar needing prayer. It was spoken over me that I was receiving a matriarch mantel anointing being passed down from generations prior.

Still very much overwhelmed in my grief, God seemed so close. The scripture, "The Lord is close to the brokenhearted and saves those who are crushed in spirit" came to my remembrance (Psalm 34:18, NIV). I can testify that in the midst of brokenness, God is faithful and present.

There were so many moments along the way through the grief that I could feel the glory of God's presence in a tangible demonstration. The word "glory" is translated as a "heavy weight." The heaviness of God's presence is so comforting. I would love to linger in His presence to feel the comfort of His Holy Spirit to my weary soul.

As time passed, the grief did not get better or easier; I just became used to the feeling of it. Every moment on this earth would continue to be so different without mom there. Charlotte's fourth birthday was on August 28th. As we tried our best to celebrate, we were all wishing mom was there to celebrate with us. Somehow I knew that all the future "happy" celebrations would always feel like something was missing. The saying, "the joy of the Lord is my strength," came to remembrance (Nehemiah 8:10, NKJV).

After the children of Israel returned to Jerusalem from exile, they were listening to the law being taught and read aloud. The Israelites were consumed with feeling criticized and were guilty, and they wept. The scripture states,

> then Nehemiah the governor, Ezra the priest and teacher of the Law, and the Levites who were instructing the people said to them all, "This day is holy to the Lord your God. Do not mourn or weep." For all the people had been weeping as they listened to the words of the Law. Nehemiah said,

"Go and enjoy choice food and sweet drinks, and send some to those who have nothing prepared. This day is holy to our Lord. Do not grieve, for the joy of the Lord is your strength."

—Nehemiah 8:9–10 (NIV)

Just as their teachers of the Word reminded the Israelites to cling to the joy of the Lord, the Bible reminds us to allow the joy of the Lord to be our strength even today. If you are reading this right now and you cannot feel joy due to your circumstance, begin to make declarations from the scriptures that God has given us. We must walk in faith by His Holy Spirit.

Now faith is the substance of things hoped for, the evidence of things not seen.

—Hebrews 11:1 (NKJV)

After Charlotte's birthday party, we started getting settled in our new home. My son has always loved water and swimming so, when we built our home, we put in a pool. Hudson would relax and seemed so at peace when he was in the water. We felt like we had our own personal paradise back in our country farmhouse. Our home is way off the road and secluded in a field surrounded by trees and blue skies. We would go and have evening swim time with the children and enjoy the beautiful sunset masterpiece that God painted in the sky. I am reminded of the day God spoke to me that He was preparing a table for me. It was not only until now that I could understand the meaning of that word.

The Lord is my shepherd; I shall not want. He maketh me to lie down in green pastures: He leads me beside the still waters. He restoreth my soul: he leads me in the paths of righteousness for his name's sake. Yea, though

I walk through the valley of the shadow of death, I will fear no evil: for thou art with me; thy rod and thy staff they comfort me. Thou prepares a table before me in the presence of mine enemies: thou anoints my head with oil; my cup runs over. Surely goodness and mercy shall follow me all the days of my life: and I will dwell in the house of the Lord for ever.

—Psalm 23 (KJV)

Even in the valley of the shadow of death, I could know that God was with me, and He was comforting me. Also, immediately after the valley of the shadow of death verse is when God says that He is preparing this table for me. Not only did God prepare this table of blessing for me while I was learning to walk through the valley of the shadow of death, but God was sitting there with me at the table—the King's table. In order to get to the table, I would have to continue to walk through the valley of the shadow of death. I could not pitch a tent in my grief and loss, or I would miss out on God's blessings. As I mentioned, God was still pouring out His blessings on our family, even in the midst of my grief. He would be faithful to His Word and His promises:

1) Lead me
2) Restore me
3) Comfort me
4) Sit with me
5) Pour out His blessings on me

As His children, we cannot let any circumstantial emotion rob our joy from the blessings God has for us.

Emotions, in general, are so important to the generations today that even in our text messages, we utilize emoji icons. According to the Oxford Languages, the definition of an emoji is "a small digital image or icon used to express an emotion."[5]

The world that you and I are living in places so much emphasis on "emotional wellbeing" with sayings like, "express yourself" and "you do you" that it can be easy to use our emotions as justification for sinful thoughts or expressions. God's Word is the most powerful source we have to combat the emotional bondage that can tie us down and paralyze us so that we are not effective in furthering the commission of God in our lives.

> Every Scripture is God-breathed (given by His inspiration) and profitable for instruction, for reproof and conviction of sin, for correction of error and discipline in obedience, for training in righteousness, so that the man of God may be complete and proficient, well fitted and thoroughly equipped for every good work.
>
> —2 Timothy 3:16-17 (AMPC)

When we get stuck in fear, anxiety, anger, bitterness, sadness, grief, and desperation, we are not just hurting ourselves; we are hindering the spread of the Gospel. These emotions can take captive of our minds and gifts and make us ineffective. The good news is that God created us as emotional beings—emotions are important, and when God helps us overcome these emotions, it becomes a part of our testimony.

Guess what? It is okay to feel whatever emotion you feel, because we should not judge our feelings. We should only fully feel them and then surrender them to God.

I know first hand it is so hard sometimes to lay down our emotional baggage and mindsets in our current culture. This is why we need to know God's Word and surround ourselves with people who can encourage and help us be victorious over our feelings. Remind yourself that victory is not a feeling; it is our position as believers. We are not moved by our feelings, we are anointed, walking in God's power, and led by His Holy Spirit.

THREATENED

In the early months of our marriage in 2009, my husband, Allen, had his first experience with a kidney stone. I will never forget—we were living in the infamous love shack at the time, I was on a Saturday shopping trip, and he called me moaning in pain. I came home and rushed him to the urgent care, and, sure enough, they said it was a kidney stone. He finally passed it but has always been cautious about them since. Every so often, he would have a pain or twinge that led him to believe there was a new stone forming or moving.

It was no surprise then that, not long after we moved into our home, Allen had another battle with kidney stone pain. He was hurting pretty bad and taking medications that had helped in the past, but getting no relief. He went to the doctor, and they told him he had a large stone that they did not think he would be able to pass on his own.

The doctor felt that Allen would need to have a procedure done in order to pass the stone. We decided to go ahead and have the recommended procedure of lithotripsy done in an attempt to crush the stone so that he could safely pass it. This was an unexpected financial hit, as well as what we felt was an attack on our family.

I was just getting tired of feeling like every time I turned around, there was another attack on my family. First, it was my son in July with a mysterious virus. Then it was my mom dying unexpectedly, then my daughter's emergency room visit, and now Allen with another kidney stone, along with a huge medical bill. Not to mention the previous medical bills from Hudson and Charlotte's hospital stays.

> The righteous cry and the LORD hears And delivers them out of all their troubles.
>
> —Psalm 34:17 (NKJV)

This is a reminder that God is all we need to overcome spiritual attacks. I was feeling discouraged, but I was thankful that Allen finally was able to pass the stone and seemed to be on the mend, improving daily.

Not long after the kidney stone escapade, on September 6, 2019, hurricane Dorian was making its way to North Carolina, and the weather was worsening as the day passed by. Schools dismissed early, businesses closed early, and even the office I worked at stopped seeing patients earlier than usual. I came home and relieved the nanny so she could get home safely.

My husband called me and said that he had a really bad headache, did not feel well, and that he was going to come home early. When he walked in, I will never forget that he was shivering and shaking, pale, and looked horrible. He was wearing his coat and still having chills. It was early September in eastern North Carolina, so we were far from fall weather. I checked his temperature, and it was over one hundred and one degrees Fahrenheit. I knew I would need to take him to the doctor somewhere.

After calling the doctor, a few calls later, and getting childcare arranged, we hurried to the nearest urgent care. Also, remember that we were in the middle of a passing hurricane with howling winds and pouring rain. My husband and I hoped that this fever was just coming from the effects of a fraction of a kidney stone blocking something and causing an infection. When we saw the doctor, Allen could barely speak for himself; he was so sick and weak. The doctor looked at me, and I just burst into tears. I was worn slam out and scared to death at the thought of something being wrong with my family rock and best friend. The doctor probably thought I was nuts until he heard the whole spill of the chaos we had been dealing with. However, he still had no answers as to why Allen was so sick. He said there was no kidney infection visible, so he recommended that we go to the nearest emergency room.

Here we go again—traveling thirty miles further, in the middle of this hurricane, needing an extended time of childcare and the fear of the unknown. After hours in the waiting room, we were finally called back. The assessment was a thorough workup. They tested him for everything from strep to flu until they decided he must have spinal meningitis. *What in the world is going on?* They put us in an isolation room and told us to be prepared to stay a few days.

Naturally, I was freaking out. We had two small children (one having special needs) staying with my aunt, who thought she would be there for an hour or two at most during the middle of a hurricane. Allen had endured a lot of testing that night, and to watch the strongest man I know suffer was awful.

We had tried to remain positive, but we were running out of positivity. Positivity and good vibes will not be what breaks chains and free you from anxiety or depression. God's Word and His presence is the only true way to be delivered from all your anguish.

> My flesh and my heart may fail, but God is the strength of my heart and my portion forever.
>
> —Psalm 73:26 (NIV)

I began to call on prayer warriors to pray for a miracle. When you are at your weakest, or you feel like you are dodging punches from the enemy at every angle; it is okay to ask for help. It is okay to ask for prayer warriors. God created people to have the gift of intercessory for a reason, and there are many people all around the world that can pray on your behalf. I truly believe in the supernatural power of the Holy Spirit.

A family member living in another state called me and began to pray with us. I put it on speakerphone, and we all prayed in the Holy Spirit. She spoke God's Word and chose to believe the report of the Lord that Allen would be healed and released so that we could go home where we needed to be.

Not long after that phone call and a change of staff from night to day shift, a team of doctors came in and said, "We think you have viral meningitis and not bacterial, so it is okay for you to go home; with time and some medications you should begin to get better." We could not believe it. The doctors completely shifted their plan of care in only a few hours. God heard our cries and prayers and answered them.

Allen was still not feeling great, but at least we no longer had to be in isolation, and we could come home to our two children. We were so thankful for God's mercy and goodness.

> You will not have to fight this battle. Take up your positions; stand firm and see the deliverance the Lord will give you.
>
> —2 Chronicles 20:17 (NIV)

Whose report will you believe? Maybe you are faced with a diagnosis, and the medical report does not look well. I encourage you even if you do not feel it, declare God's Word out loud, call on believers to help you, and stand on His Word. We can be like David when he said:

> Your word is a lamp to guide my feet and a light for my path. I've promised it once, and I'll promise it again: I will obey your righteous regulations... The wicked have set their traps for me, but I will not turn from your commandments. Your laws are my treasure; they are my heart's delight.
>
> —Psalms 119:105-106, 110-111 (NLT)

My birthday and our tenth anniversary were only days after our hospital experience. Originally, we had grand plans to renew our vows on the front steps of our new home, but instead, I would be trying to nurse my husband back to health so he could recover from meningitis. "In sickness and in health" are true vows. I missed my mom's annual birthday song call, as well as her special birthday trips and treats. My mom's extravagant tastes were always deemed for a girl's day trip to the mall. I missed that sweet precious time so much.

Shortly after mom passed away, my grandmother told me of a package that shipped to her house that mom would want me to have. To my surprise, my mom's grand gift was a brand new designer pocketbook. It was very unlike my mom to plan ahead gifts, but this year was different. Even though she was not able to be with me on my birthday this year, she would make sure I received the best gift. She always knew my frugal nature would be that I would never buy myself such a luxurious gift. She spoiled me even from heaven.

Do not misunderstand me though; gifts are no replacement for the love and life of a parent or any person. I will always miss my mother, and this gift was another reminder of her extravagance.

My family and I were still getting adjusted to our new normal; weekly Sunday lunches after church were never the same, and we continued to try to make them as special as she always did. My siblings and I, still to this day, rely on the support of one another.

Work for me was going well; I was succeeding in all areas of my work. I was told I would receive a bonus in the new year, and I was so grateful. Our company was merging with other companies, and our benefits would be better and more affordable. They were working in an effort to bring more unity and leadership in our workplace. Honestly, I was in a really good spot in my career. I rubbed elbows, so to speak, with many of the leaders within the organization, because I had been with the company for about twelve years. I loved my boss and my employees. Even through my grief and chaos, I seemed to be thriving in the workplace.

Allen was doing well at work also, and our nanny was amazing at taking care of our children. We were able to get Charlotte into the same preschool as our son so that she could get a more formal education. Things seemed to be looking up for us. For the first time in my career, my income would be at an all-time high. Surely we could pay off some of these hospital bills and settle into our new home.

UNQUALIFIED

Life seemed to be going in fast forward as my timeline jumped from one chaotic moment to the next. Even the happy times seemed chaotic to me because I was still learning to cope with my own depression and anxiety, as well as be the "matriarch" for my family. Hudson's sixth birthday was in November, another birthday and yet another reminder of my mom's absence. *How could our miracle baby boy be turning six years old? Where did the time go? God, why has Hudson not overcome the diagnosis of autism yet? When will I hear my son's voice again? Why didn't mom get to see him healed?* These are questions that I still do not have the answers to. I know one thing, though; I know God birthed the promise that Hudson would speak.

God is faithful to His promises. I know God will allow our son to speak and use his voice to testify of God's miracle-working power. God has given my family several specific dreams of Hudson speaking, and I will not lose faith. Whatever it looks like, whatever it sounds like. God's Word tells me that He has plans to prosper Hudson and not to harm him to give him a hope and a future (see Jeremiah 29:11, NIV). He that began a good work in Hudson is faithful to complete it.

> Being confident of this very thing, that He who has begun a good work in you will complete it until the day of Jesus Christ.
>
> —Philippians 1:6 (NIV)

The journey that we are on with autism may not be easy, but it is beautiful. I must continue to trust God and keep His Word constantly in front of my face and in my heart in order to keep going. Never lose faith in your own journey; never stop dreaming and never give up. The Word of God is the light and when you are learning to shine even in the midst of darkness, you will have to hide His Word in your heart.

The light shines in the darkness, and the darkness has not overcome it.

—John 1:5 (NIV)

Darkness cannot consume your emotions, your joy, or your strength if you allow the light of God's Word to flood your soul. My prayer is that you will find something in my story to relate to, but mostly that you would find hope and faith in the Gospel of Jesus Christ. We will be overcomers by the blood of the Lamb and the word of our testimonies. God's Word is sharper than any two-edged sword—friend, it is all you need to live and shine in this dark world.

After I was just getting used to the routine of living our new normal, I had this feeling in my spirit that something was about to change, but I could not put my finger on it. I, of course, feared change, though, because I feared the pain of any more heartache. I remember telling my husband that something just seemed out of place or that it would change soon. In December, my children were about to go on Christmas break from school, and I got a message from our nanny saying that she wanted to talk to me that evening when I got home from work. I had that sick feeling in my stomach, and I knew change was on the way.

When I got home, we talked; as soon as she told me she was going to be taking a job in a school, I wept. Through all the chaos since mom's unexpected death, the nanny had been the only constant. I felt like my world was being turned upside down. It was extremely hard to find someone like our nanny that could handle the rigorous schedules, therapies for Hudson, and extensive transportation time in the car. I knew deep down we would never find someone to replace her, and I also knew deep down I needed to come home.

This sudden change would happen immediately after Christmas, and so it would require a quick turnaround. When I told Allen the news he said, "Okay, I have peace about it." I was so surprised because I had no peace about it. I was sick to my stomach. We brainstormed for days during Christmas break, trying to think of a solution.

Have you ever felt this calling to do something completely off-course of what you planned? This is where I was. I felt the need to fast in order to hear God's voice and know without a shadow of a doubt what He was calling me to do. I chose to go on a twenty-one day fast in the New Year. I am also someone who takes a long time to make big decisions. I remember I was searching for scriptures and prayers to pray so that I could clearly hear the voice of God. Daniel chapter nine became my personal anthem and favorite passage. During this time, Daniel prayed and fasted for three weeks or twenty-one days. He asked the Lord to have mercy on him and to give him a clear understanding.

> While I was speaking and praying, confessing my sin and the sin of my people Israel and making my request to the Lord my God for his holy hill while I was still in prayer, Gabriel, the man I had seen in the earlier vision, came to me in swift flight about the time of the evening sacrifice. He instructed me and said to me, "Daniel, I have now come to give you insight and understanding. As soon as you began to pray, a word went out, which I have come to tell you, for you are highly esteemed. Therefore, consider the word and understand the vision."
>
> —Daniel 9:20-23 (NIV)

When Daniel cried out, God sent Gabriel to give him insight and understanding. God's Word is not dead; that is why He is called "The Living God". If God could bring understanding and insight to Daniel, then He could do the same for me. Even still, my flesh was weak, and I would wrestle with my flesh daily, trying to talk myself out of leaving my amazing career and choosing to come home and be a stay-at-home mom.

I was even so eager to drag this thing out that I broke up my fast into twenty-one days of total fasting that lasted until March of 2020. During this time, we were able to receive some help from a family member who cared for our children. Even still, I kept praying for signs or an audible voice from God. One day, our new nanny and close family member called me and said that she had been in a minor car accident in our vehicle, but our car would have to be towed. Thankfully, the children were not in the car, and she was not injured. I really felt like God was saying, "Okay, Lindsay, how many more signs do you need?"

In my doubt and stubbornness, I still resisted God's calling. Early in my fast, I felt the urge to quit my job. I wanted to talk about my possible resignation to my boss and the physician I worked closely with. They were supportive and were agreeable to work with me and my work schedule so that I could be more available for the children, but hopefully not have to quit. They were so gracious in doing that for me, and it made me feel valued as an employee. That seemed like the best of both worlds, right?

Well, sometimes God wants total obedience because He has greater plans for our lives. Even though I knew what God wanted me to do, I still tried to make it work with partial obedience. I did all the transportation, and the nanny just kept the children when they were not at school. Thankfully, my boss was a spirit-filled believer and she would check in with me daily and ask how things were going. I poured my heart out to her and asked her to pray about it. One day, she called me, and I asked her again like I always did to pray that God would reveal the answer to me and she said she knew the answer. She said she knew all along that God was calling me home, but she hated to lose me as an employee. I revealed to her that I already knew that as well, yet selfishly, I wanted to make both options work.

Our new nanny knew my petition to God, and she was also praying with me for direction. She loved taking care of our children, and she was good at it. God began to speak to her as well. You see, God's relentless love was so strong for me and my desire to make His direction clear in my life that not only did He begin to confirm His affirmation to me, but He also confirmed it to my boss and the new nanny. The nanny was fasting and praying as well for direction in her own life. One day, I came home from work and she told me, "As bad as I want to be here, I feel like I am doing your job." This spoke volumes to me, and I felt like God was using a megaphone and saying once more, "Just trust me."

On March 2nd, I handed in a written letter of resignation as a thirty-day notice. Just about this time, the global pandemic was making its way into the United States of America. Roars of fear and anxiety seemed to be flooding our nation. Plans for the healthcare industry were changing daily. I honestly did not understand the timing of this personal decision in the midst of this global crisis. The whole world was in chaos, people were scared to death, and people were dying everyday. Schools began closing, and there was no end in sight. As confident as I finally was in my decision to leave my workplace, I still was so heartbroken to see my work family have to deal with this crisis without me. I also had a lot of anxiety about becoming a stay at home mom since this would be an entirely new world for me. I felt unqualified for the task that God was calling me to, but I knew Him as the one who equips the unarmed, weakest, and least likely to succeed.

> Not that we are sufficient in ourselves to claim anything as coming from us, but our sufficiency is from God.
>
> —2 Corinthians 3:5 (NIV)

One day while I was praying in the prayer closet, I begged God to reveal to me what my role was during the global pandemic, and while I was still working out the rest of my notice at work. God immediately spoke the word "glitter" to me. I did not doubt this word, but I thought, *you know, maybe I am losing my mind.* Would it be justifiable after all I have been through in the last year? Again, God spoke "glitter" to my spirit. I remember asking what in the world is biblical about glitter. God said, "Be the glitter, shine My light." I believe God speaks to us in ways that we will understand. I always have loved glitter—the sparkle, the shine, the extravagance of glitter. In fact, I already owned several clothing items that had glitter on them, and in stores I am always drawn to the most unique items, especially if they sparkle.

God spoke to my spirit and brought the scripture to my remembrance that states,

You are the light of the world. A town built on a hill cannot be hidden. Neither do people light a lamp and put it under a bowl. Instead they put it on its stand, and it gives light to everyone in the house. In the same way, let your light shine before others, that they may see your good deeds and glorify your Father in heaven.

— Matthew 5:14-16 (NIV)

I knew that in my workplace, there was a lot of unrest, anxiety, and fear surfacing and seemingly dominating the atmosphere. At that moment, I felt like glitter was a timely word because while I did not have the answers on the best protocols or procedures to handle the current pandemic. I could, however, share the truth of what God's Word says. I had to be the positive light radiating God's love so that his people could still trust him.

It does not matter where you are in life or what your circumstances are if you have Jesus Christ as your Lord and Savior, then you have His light in your life. As your relationship deepens with Him, you will bear much fruit. The Bible says that people will be known by their fruit (see Matthew 7:16-20, NKJV).

Every morning at work, we made the decision to have daily huddles. I chose to request at this time to say a prayer each day that God would be in control. I did not work in a Christian workplace, but no one objected to my request, and I prayed. People that knew God and people who did not know Him began to weep during the prayer. The Bible also says that he would draw all men unto him (see John 12:32, KJV). The Holy Spirit is just as contagious as the virus. What greater hope can we share then the hope of Jesus Christ?

"Yet a little while is the light with you. Walk while ye have the light, lest darkness come upon you: for he that walketh in darkness knoweth not whither he goeth."

—John 12:35 (KJV)

In that moment of huddle prayer, people felt faith rise over their fear.

As Christians, we have the comfort of the Holy Spirit that the world needs. I want to be obedient to the calling God has on my life, and I pray you choose to as well. Remember the Great Commission:

> Then Jesus came to them and said, "All authority in heaven and on earth has been given to me. Therefore go and make disciples of all nations, baptizing them in the name of the Father and of the Son and of the Holy Spirit, and teaching them to obey everything I have commanded you. And surely I am with you always, to the very end of the age."
>
> —Matthew 28:18-20 (NIV)

People will always be drawn to the light. If you are reading this right now, then God has chosen you to be a lampstand, a light in the dark world, the glitter so to speak. Do not be ashamed of the Gospel,

> but if anyone suffers as a Christian, he is not to be ashamed, but is to glorify God in this name.
>
> —1 Peter 4:16 (NASB)

God has never promised that the walk would be easy, but He has promised to be right beside us.

AFFIRMED

The first of April came quickly, and it was my last day of work. My children were already at home because their preschool, like most all schools, did not feel it was safe to continue during the peak of the virus. I quickly had to become acclimated as a preschool teacher, speech therapist, and adjust to the new role of stay at home mom. We were quarantined and dependent on grocery deliveries, online education, and services of all kinds.

I never thought my son's last semester of the autism program would be like this. He had been at this school for three years, and I felt like he would not get the most of his experience or have the graduation we planned. I know this may seem shallow because of all the other suffering in the world at this time, but I grieved his experience for him. I wanted him to know how proud we all were of him, and I wanted to know that he knew everything he needed to know before kindergarten. Suddenly, I felt unqualified again and in addition, a heavy sense of responsibility for his education. Cooking three meals a day, taking care of two children trapped inside a house, trying to teach, and doing speech therapy were none of my areas of expertise.

As I came more and more into a routine, I realized how lonely stay at home moms can feel at times. You have no other adults to interact with and, during this time of quarantine, I could not even have visitors because of the pandemic. I was also still grieving the loss of my mother. I became totally dependent on the comfort of the Holy Spirit.

April fifteenth was my mom's first heavenly birthday. That morning, while we were following our daily schedule, Charlotte and I sat at the breakfast table together. I had tears welled in my eyes as I reflected on all that had happened and mourning and missing my mom.

About this time, Charlotte looked over at me and said, "Mommy, there is a man sitting beside you."

I was a little freaked out naturally, but also thought that Charlotte may have been just utilizing her very creative imagination. I said, "Are you just pretending?"

She said, "No, Mommy, there is a man sitting beside you with white hair, and He looks like an angel."

Immediately, in my spirit I felt God speak and say, "It is okay to feel sad, but know that I am right beside you." I actually had my Bible on the table and it was already open. I looked down, and it was open to that familiar scripture,

> The Lord is close to the brokenhearted and saves those who are crushed in spirit.
>
> —Psalm 34:18 (NIV)

How amazing that God took a moment to comfort me with His presence even though there were so many more important things going on in the world.

You see, that is why I felt the urgency and desire to reference emotions throughout this book. God is omnipresent, everywhere at the same time, yet He cared so much about each emotion that I have experienced just in the last few years that He rescued me from the captivity of those emotions.

Like I have said earlier, God made us uniquely different, but He made us all emotional beings. Maybe you are feeling guilty for having fluctuating emotions or unrest at where you are in your own walk with Christ. If you are that one, I can attest that God's love and desire for your soul is relentless. He loves you. All you have to do is accept Jesus as your Lord and Savior, and surrender to Him and His calling on your life.

Leave your past behind; God has forgiven you of your sins. The Bible is jam-packed with promises of God's forgiveness—He will remember your sins no more.

As far as the east is from the west, so far has he removed our transgressions from us. As a father has compassion on his children, so the LORD has compassion on those who fear him.

—Psalm 103:12-13 (NIV)

If we confess our sins, he is faithful and just and will forgive us our sins and purify us from all unrighteousness.

—1 John 1:9 (NIV)

"Their sins and lawless acts I will remember no more."

—Hebrews 10:17 (NIV)

On April fifteenth, I was blown away that God would sit with me in my heartache. Even though I could not see Him with my eyes, I was reminded that He is always with me.

During my time of quarantine and adjusting to my new roles and responsibilities, I pondered on scriptures and dreams that seemed to have died years ago. You can ask my husband and he will tell you that I have always been a dreamer and not a realist. Every time I would dedicate time to spend in God's presence, He would renew my mind and resurrect dreams that I thought were dead.

I have always had the desire to write a book, but I have never felt qualified. I also never knew what that book would even look like. One night it was like God connected the dots in my dreams and timeline. He gave me this title, *Gospel Glitter*.

I realized that the only thing that has carried me in trials and seasons of my life had been the living Word of God.

For the Word of God is living and powerful, and sharper than any two-edged sword, piercing even to the division of soul and spirit, and of joints and marrow, and is a discerner of the thoughts and intents of the heart.

—Hebrews 4:12 (KJV)

My story and survival strategy was too good not to share with others. I knew that if I was feeling these emotions and struggling to know God's voice, then there were probably others. God began to affirm this desire in my heart continually through wise counsel. Even though I have felt unqualified in so many ways for so many roles, God still called me and chose me to be a witness and a vessel of His unfailing love.

Throughout my life and seasons of trials and suffering through loss and emotional turmoil, I have recognized God's faithfulness. My journey is not over; it may just be beginning, but I know that I serve a good God that I can trust with my life and my family's lives. The best is yet to come.

If you are reading this book, then God is drawing you to Him and His Word. I pray the Word of God begins to illuminate in your Bible and in your life. Even in a global quarantine movement, you are not meant to go through life alone.

> And let us consider how we may spur one another on toward love and good deeds, not giving up meeting together, as some are in the habit of doing, but encouraging one another—and all the more as you see the Day approaching.
>
> —Hebrews 10:24-25 (NIV)

I want to encourage you, friends, that the day is approaching when Jesus is coming back to rapture the Church.

> For we believe that Jesus died and rose again, and so we believe that God will bring with Jesus those who have fallen asleep in him. According to the Lord's word, we

tell you that we who are still alive, who are left until the coming of the Lord, will certainly not precede those who have fallen asleep. For the Lord himself will come down from heaven, with a loud command, with the voice of the archangel and with the trumpet call of God, and the dead in Christ will rise first. After that, we who are still alive and are left will be caught up together with them in the clouds to meet the Lord in the air. And so we will be with the Lord forever. Therefore encourage one another with these words.

—1 Thessalonians 4:14-18 (NIV)

The hope and promise of the Gospel must be spread to the ends of the earth. Rejoice that God chose you to reach the harvest during this season.

But you are a chosen people, a royal priesthood, a holy nation, God's special possession, that you may declare the praises of him who called you out of darkness into his wonderful light.

—1 Peter 2:9 (NIV)

EPILOGUE

The year 2020 quickly proved to be a challenge to the entire world. The evident darkness of evil caused a global wave of fear and destruction. Not only has everyday life been a challenge, but it has also wreaked havoc on the emotional wellbeing of our brothers and sisters in Christ. One moment in the presence of God revealed to me a calling and a purpose.

To be like glitter is to be a bright light, shining, difficult to wipe out, and contagious to all of mankind. *Gospel Glitter* will be an additional method of delivering hope and encouragement to this generation and generations to come. As you have now seen the power and impact that the Word of God has had in my life, I pray you are motivated to join this glitter movement with me, to make a global impact, and further the Great Commission.

> Then Jesus came to them and said, "All authority in heaven and on earth has been given to me. Therefore go and make disciples of all nations, baptizing them in the name of the Father and of the Son and of the Holy Spirit, and teaching them to obey everything I have commanded you. And surely I am with you always, to the very end of the age."
>
> —Matthew 28:16-20 (NIV)

Gospel Glitter began as seemingly endless journal entries of prayer requests, scriptures, and a log of answered prayers and victories throughout my life. I believed that a therapeutic survival strategy and testament of the faithfulness and goodness of God was never meant to gather dust in my closet. To share my personal journey through myriad trials and sufferings is a raw exposure in an effort to overcome the darkness that may surround me from time to time. This story is still not completed, so stay tuned for more evidence of the miracle working power of God the Father, the Son, and the Holy Spirit. I profess to leave a legacy by learning to shine the light of Christ in the darkness.

Let the Word of God be illuminated to you and in you and never forget to share the light of the Gospel. Join the #gospelglitter movement with me, and let's shine the light for all the world to see!

AUTHOR'S NOTE

As a new and aspiring author, I am humbled and honored that God would allow me to be a useful vessel for His eternal kingdom's furtherment. Since I was a little girl, I have always had a deep desire to serve God in a big way. I have always desired to make a global impact by sharing the Gospel of Jesus Christ. My journey has not always been easy, but God has always guided me through with His Word.

I believe that I have marching orders or, in other words, a direct mission from God. Obedience to God, even in the midst of uncertainties, may be considered a leap of faith to most. I believe that obedience will propel believers like me to their destinies as children of God. We were all made for kingdom growth and a relationship with Christ.

Praise God for giving His only son Jesus as a sacrifice to save a wretch like me. I may be unworthy, but by His redemptive grace, forgiveness, and sanctification, I am free from the chains of this world. I am thankful for a Christian heritage and a supportive husband and family. I give God all the glory, honor, and praise for this simple testament of His faithfulness and goodness in my own life.

I am excited to witness a great awakening of God's people and a revival through worship and declaring the promises of God from His Gospel. Miracles and wonders are still in store for those that put their faith, hope, and trust in Him.

Blessings,

Lindsay Stone Corbett

AUTHOR'S BIBLIOGRAPHY

Lindsay Stone Corbett was born in rural eastern North Carolina to Daryl and Sandy Stone. Lindsay pursued a career as a nurse and graduated from East Carolina University in Greenville, North Carolina, with a bachelor of science degree in nursing in 2007. From 2007-2020, Lindsay worked as an RN (registered nurse).

In 2009, Lindsay married John "Allen" Corbett III, and they have two beautiful children—Hudson and Charlotte. Lindsay has been a faithful and serving member of her home church, Midpoint Church (formerly Middlesex Church of God), since 1985. She has served in children's, youth, couples', and women's ministries. Her newest adventures consist of being a full-time mom, currently home-schooling, and becoming a new and aspiring author.

Lindsay loves the Lord with all her heart, and is a willing vessel birthed with a vision for global impact through her new book, Gospel Glitter. Lindsay's heart is drawn to parents and women who have faced infertility, infant loss, and parents of children with special needs. Lindsay believes that the Bible is breathed directly from God, and the promises from the past are still available to us today. She believes salvation is God's best gift to us as believers, but telling our story to give hope and faith to others is a believer's best gift back to God.

ENDNOTES

[1] Merriam-Webster Dictionary, s.v. "Glitter". <https://www.merriam-webster.com/dictionary/glitter>

[2] Merriam-Webster Dictionary, s.v. "Surprise". <https://www.merriam-webster.com/dictionary/surprise>

[3] Joyce Meyer Ministries. "In His Image: Daily Devo." Joyce Meyer Ministries, joycemeyer.org dailydevo/2020/08/0822-in-his-image.

[4] Merriam-Webster Dictionary, s.v. "Guilt".

[5] Oxford Dictionary, s.v. "emoji".

CPSIA information can be obtained
at www.ICGtesting.com
Printed in the USA
BVHW050519050522
635937BV00005B/15